IMPROVE YOUR EYESIGHT — GET YOUR EYES SHIFTING AGAIN

START NOW WITH THIS QUICK ACTION GUIDE

GLORIA GINN

JGF Press

Published in the United States by JGF Press
First publication: July 1, 2019 as *You CAN Improve Your Eyesight: Here's How*
Revised, expanded and re-titled on May 10, 2021

Limit of Liability / Disclaimer: This publication does not provide medical advice. Its contents, such as text, graphics, images and other material are for informational purposes only are are not intended to be a substitute for professional medical advice, diagnosis or treatment. Always seek the advice of your physician or other qualified health provider with any questions you may have regarding a medical condition. Never disregard professional medical advice or delay in seeking it because of something you have read.

The author and publisher specifically disclaim any responsibility for any liability, loss, or risk, personal or otherwise, which is incurred as a consequence, directly or indirectly, of the use and application of any of the contents of this publication.

Photo Credits:

- **Front cover** and all interior photos which are not specifically credited to another source are by *Gloria Ginn.*

- **Back cover** (print edition) dark blue starry sky full page photo by *José Reyes* on *Unsplash*. Portrait of Gloria Ginn by *Lewisburg Studio*.
- ***Artwork***: Illustrations of the eyeball are by *Emily Mills* at https://emilyamills.com.

HERE'S WHAT READERS SAY

"Gloria Ginn has a unique method of teaching which is reflected in this book. The most important part of this method can be summed up in one word: *Results*.

"While some people merely inspire and paint pictures of possibilities, Ginn actually gets you where you want to go, in a clear, simple and effective way. The techniques laid out in this book have helped me become a more relaxed and confident person, with the added benefit of being able to see clearly again."

STEVEN SPRUNG, NEW MEXICO

From being a Braille student diagnosed with the irreversible wet macular degeneration and preparing to be partially sighted if not blind, I now see 20/40 and 20/30 because Gloria Ginn taught me specific ways to relax and exercise my eyes' ability to see whatever they are attracted to see.

PATRICIA S., SANTA MONICA, CALIFORNIA

"I've been utilizing this book for quite some time and it has proven to assist me in improving my eyesight quickly, from the very beginning.

"It has also continued to help me improve my visual clarity since that initial start.

"Gloria is precise, exceptionally effective within her work as a coach helping people improve their vision, and is typically very concise with her words. She's got an amazing ability to deliver the nuggets that matter most with extraordinary efficiency.

"The material in this book allowed me to gain improvement quickly with my vision. Its potential doesn't end with an initial quick start, however. I've also come back to this book repeatedly, utilized it while doing some of the vision improvement exercises themselves, and have gained tremendous insights that have expanded the improvement of my vision clarity since my favorable beginning with it.

"This title is a must-have for anyone serious about improving their vision. In fact, in my opinion, Gloria Ginn is a must-have in a coach for anyone serious about improving their vision. Not all material out there, nor all teachers on the subject, are able to deliver the results Gloria typically helps people achieve."

HOLLY FISCHER, NEW YORK

"The writing has been really helpful. Every time I re-read it, I get a deeper and better understanding of what Gloria had taught us.

"My confidence arises significantly when I realize that whatever Gloria taught and wrote is so consistent. Yes, I know the reason behind my eye sight problem and I am on my way to regain my 20/20 vision soon."

JUNE TAN, MALAYSIA

"I keep coming back to Gloria's book. She distills the core principles of the Bates Method of Natural vision, and provides specific practices for each of these principles. It is a streamlined example of putting theory into practice. Thank you Gloria for sharing your wisdom so succinctly."

EVELYN A., ENGLAND

"Gloria is a magician! When I first took her "21 Day Challenge: Read Without Glasses," I was wearing +6.5 and +5.5 diopter glasses. By the 16th day, I had read a whole page with just my own two eyes. After 41 years in the glasses club, it took just 2 months to put them aside. I am still working with Gloria, but I have come such a long way with her patient, kind, and knowledgeable teaching abilities."

SAPNA, FORT COLLINS, COLORADO

FOREWORD

BY GLORIA GINN

How can you improve eyesight in the fastest, easiest way? This question has been the driving force behind my work for over 45 years.

When I began in 1978 as a newly-minted certified teacher of the Bates-Corbett[1] method, I realized very quickly that I had hundreds of techniques but no clear understanding of how and when to use them.

Sometimes a technique would work extremely well — and sometimes not.

RESULTS ARE OBVIOUS AND MEASURABLE

This method is not subjective: Results are obvious. You either see a smaller line of letters — or not. You read smaller size text — or not. If a technique is working, it is obvious immediately, instantly.

This fact makes the method exciting and dynamic: There

is nothing like the joy of seeing the vision clear up right before your eyes.

It can also be frustrating when a technique doesn't work — the failure is obvious too. This fact put a lot of pressure on me as a new teacher. I would try one of the techniques, and if it didn't work I would scramble to find a technique that would. Sometimes I went through quite a few before stumbling on one that was successful.

Afterward, I would analyze the lesson to try to figure out why the one technique didn't work, and why another one did. Why one cleared up the vision, and the other didn't.

Over a period of many years, working with thousands of students, I gained more skill in being able to quickly discard techniques that don't work, and isolate those that do — for each person. These days, I am confident that when a client walks in my door, he/she will walk out with better vision after that first lesson.

DON'T STRUGGLE WITH TECHNIQUES THAT DON'T WORK

It is always best to focus on the techniques that give you immediate improvement. Don't waste time with others. As Dr. Bates so aptly said, "The cause of failure is strain, and it does no good to go on straining."

What if none of the techniques work for you? Usually that is because of one of two things:

1. You are not applying the technique properly. This is likely when you are working on your own,

without supervision. Why? Because if you have imperfect sight you have a habit of straining to see. Chances are pretty high that you will apply the same strain when trying to improve your vision. Look at Part II in this book on the *Four Keys to Success*. These tips can help you get past the habit of straining, so that the techniques begin to sharpen up your vision.
2. You are not practicing under favorable conditions. If you are using letter charts, put them at the distance where they are just slightly out of focus, instead of all the way across the room. Practice in sunlight, instead of in a dark room. See Chapter 3 for more tips to make your practice successful.

If you still do not see results, get help. Why struggle with things that don't work? Try a few fixes, and if you can't do it yourself, get someone to help you. Just like contacting technical support when you are stuck with a computer glitch, an expert can save you hours of time and a lot of frustration. (I have Apple Support on my "speed dial.") You can put me on your "speed dial" here: School of Better Eyesight Booking Site.

When you get more experience, many of the techniques that don't work for you right now *will* begin to work, as you learn how to relax and focus your attention more clearly. But in the first few stages of vision improvement, it is essential to use your most favorable techniques, under the most favorable conditions.

(The concept of favorable conditions is a book all by itself.

Yes, I've written it, but it is not available to the public right now.)

Advice? Have fun improving your vision! Enjoy the improved clarity you experience — both visually and mentally. And re-claim the perfect sight that is your birthright.

INTRODUCTION: THE THREE HABITS OF THE NORMAL EYE

WHEN THESE HABITS ARE RE-ESTABLISHED, NORMAL SIGHT RETURNS

Why is it that some people keep perfect sight all their lives, while others lose it in the first grade?

The difference is in the mind, for strange as it may sound, vision is 9/10ths mental and only 1/10th physical. Most vision problems are not caused by a physical disability of the eye, but are simply the result of an unconscious mental strain to see.

WHAT PRODUCES GOOD VISION

The person with normal sight unconsciously practices certain mental habits of seeing that the person with imperfect sight fails to practice. When these habits are reestablished, normal sight returns.

Thousands of people have used this method to regain perfect sight. And you can, too.

THE HABITS OF THE NORMAL EYE

There are three habits of the normal eye::

1. **Motion**: *Shifting* and *Swinging*
2. **Effortless focus**: *Rest* and *Central Fixation*
3. **Mental pictures**: *Memory* and *Imagination*

When one of these habits is present, the others are also present to the same degree. So you can develop the one(s) easiest for you, and the others follow.

1. MOTION: *SHIFTING* AND *SWINGING*

Motion consists of two elements: shifting and swinging. Shifting is what the eyes do. They shift, or scan 70-100 times per second with normal sight.

Swinging is what objects looks like when your eyes shift: Objects appear to move, or ***swing***, in the opposite direction to the movement of the eyes. This sense of motion is your clue you are shifting correctly.

Throughout the day, when you shift your gaze from one detail to another, see all the points in between, and notice the apparent motion, or swing, that occurs.

As your vision improves, you will be able to see stationary objects moving with a short, slow, pendulum-like motion even when you are not consciously shifting. This is the ***optical swing***, and it is the final goal of motion.

2. EFFORTLESS FOCUS: *REST* AND *CENTRAL FIXATION*

"The sole cause of all uncomplicated or functional errors of refraction is a conscious or unconscious effort or strain to see. The only remedy for this strain is relaxation. Relaxation or rest of the eye is accomplished only by central fixation." — *W. H. Bates, MD*

Perfect sight requires no effort. When the sight is normal, the person sees a wide field of vision with only one tiny point in the center seen with maximum detail. This clarity of detail can only be maintained for a fraction of a second without shifting.

With imperfect sight the field of vision is narrowed, and the central clarity is lost. It is only possible to see with this clarity of focus when there is absolutely no effort to see — either consciously or unconsciously. Rest obtained through central fixation allows perfect sight to occur.

To regain the habit of effortless focus, release strain by seeing from the back of the head, and then open up your peripheral vision; don't block out any of the field of vision.

After the peripheral vision has been established and strain lowered, begin to differentiate the detail from its periphery by seeing the center point best and the periphery worse, until you can see one part of one letter best at a time at any distance.

3. MENTAL PICTURES: *MEMORY* AND *IMAGINATION*

A clear mental picture remembered or imagined produces perfect sight. That's because both perfect memory and perfect sight require the state of mind of perfect relaxation.

Imperfect sight requires a mental strain. Since the mind cannot strain and relax at the same time, when you have a clear mental picture (which is indicative of mental relaxation), you cannot have imperfect sight.

Because of the connection between memory, imagination and vision, you can use mental pictures to regain perfect sight. Cultivate your memory with the eyes open and closed. When reading, imagine a thin white line under the letters.

Vision improves the instant you practice one of these habits. By consciously imitating them until they become automatic, your vision becomes continuously good.

PART ONE
HOW TO GET STARTED IMPROVING YOUR EYESIGHT
TECHNIQUES YOU CAN APPLY IMMEDIATELY

CHAPTER 1
GETTING YOUR EYES SHIFTING AGAIN
WITHOUT SHIFTING, YOU ARE WASTING YOUR TIME

The shifter is the fastest way to break up the stare and get your eyes shifting again.

Stop Staring – Start Shifting!

"All persons with imperfect sight make an effort to stare with their eyes immovable. The eyes have not the ability to

> keep stationary. To look intently at a point continuously is impossible; the eyes will move, the eyelids will blink, and the effort is accompanied by imperfect vision.
>
> "All persons with normal sight do not concentrate or try to see by any effort. Their eyes are at rest, and when the eyes are at rest they are constantly moving."
>
> WILLIAM H. BATES, MD

If you have imperfect sight, you are staring. The eyes are stopping too long on one spot, causing a blur. You may not be staring **consciously**, but you ***are*** staring unconsciously. It has become an unconscious habit.

To improve your eyesight, you need to stop staring and start shifting. Moving your eyes consciously won't help. The eye with normal sight shifts, or scans, 70 to 100 times **every second**.

The faster the shift and the smaller the shift, the better the vision.

Obviously, if you move your eyes consciously, you will not be able to move them that fast. Consciously moving your eyes only slows down the movement.

So how do you get the eyes moving unconsciously? Fortunately, there are four techniques that have proven to be effective for this:

1. Shifter
2. Head Swing
3. Sway
4. Long Swing

These techniques can help you break up the stare and reestablish the unconscious shifting pattern of the normal eye.

LEARN THE SKILL: HOW TO USE A SHIFTER

The easiest way to break the stare, initially, is to use a shifter with the eyes closed in the sun or with a bright light.

Shift in the sun with the eyes closed. Photo by Sarah English.

1. Place the shifter between your face and the sun, long side parallel to the ground.
2. Allow the sun to shine through the holes onto your closed eyelids. Closing your eyes makes it easier to stop trying to see — and it is the effort to see that causes the stare and blurred vision.

3. Move the head alternately from left to right, while at the same time you move the shifter in the opposite direction. When the head moves to the right, the shifter moves to the left.

To use a shifter, close the eyes and move the head from left to right while you move the shifter in the opposite direction, so the sun's rays fall through the shifter onto your closed eyelids.

You can also use the shifter vertically. Move the head up while you move the shifter down, and vice versa.

Because the eyes are light-finders, they shift over the black slats in the shifter and look for the light coming through the holes. You don't have to do anything; the shifting begins automatically.

The shifter can also be used vertically (*see image*). Move the head down as you move the shifter up, and vice versa.

USING A SHIFTER WITHOUT SUN

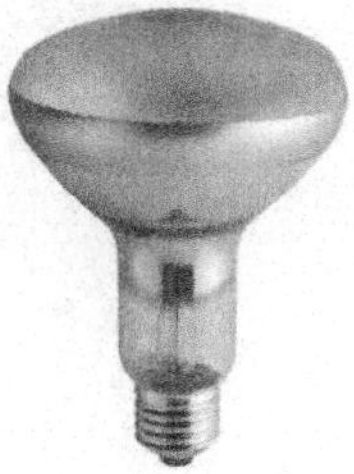

The Verilux "full-spectrum" light works well for shifting when there is no sun.

When sunlight is not available, you can use an electric light instead. The best one for this purpose is a 100 watt reflector made by Chromalux or Verilux. At the present time here are some sources for these lights:

Verilux Light Bulb from Tools for Wellness

Chromalux 100 watt full spectrum light from Chewy.com

Chromalux 100 watt full spectrum light from TractorSupply.com

Chromalux Light Bulb from uk.vitamingrocer.com

USING A SHIFTER WITHOUT A LIGHT

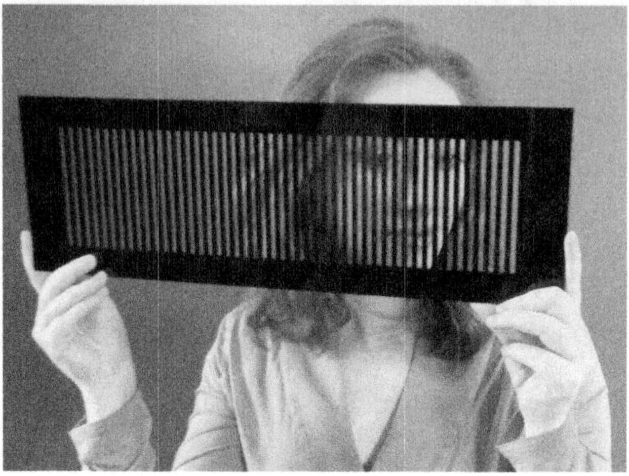

You can also use the shifter without a light, with the eyes open. The head and eyes move to the left when the shifter moves to the right, and vice versa.

You can use the shifter without the sun or a bright light — anytime, anyplace, day or night.

When shifting without a light, keep your eyes open. The head and eyes move to the left while the shifter moves to the right, and vice versa.

There should be ambient light to give the eyes something to see as they shift across the scene. The actual level of light doesn't matter; it may be bright or dim.

WHERE YOU CAN GET A SHIFTER

Please go to: https://improvesight.com/shop/

Hold the shifter very close to the face, only an inch or two away, and high enough so that the sunlight comes through the slats onto your closed eyelids.

TIPS FOR USING A SHIFTER

- Move the head and shifter **slowly**, so that the flickering light of the sun comes through the slats.
- The speed is approximately as if you would count "1, 2" as you move the head to the right and "3, 4" as you move to the left.
- It is important to move **both** the head and the shifter. The head swing by itself stimulates the involuntary shifting of the eyes. When the shifter is used, the effect is magnified.
- Hold the shifter close to the face. Almost touch the forehead with it. It is much more effective that way. You'll also find it easier to get the sun's rays to come through the slats.

- Be sure the sunlight penetrates the slats in the shifter. You may have to hold it higher up toward your hairline than you would anticipate.

HOW MUCH TIME SHOULD YOU PRACTICE WITH A SHIFTER?

Use a shifter for 5-20 minutes, once or twice per day. If you want faster improvement, shift for a half hour up to three times daily.

Years ago, I had a client who came to see me from New York City, to my office in Los Angeles. He had experienced a lot of problems with his body — three heart bypass surgeries, several retina surgeries, and was depressed about it all.

We did several lessons over a five day period, he had good results, but then went back to New York and — due to his depression — he didn't practice any of the techniques he had learned.

But the concepts made sense to him, and he kept telling his friends all about it. Finally, after about six months of this, one of his friends said, "If you think it is so good why don't you ***DO*** it?"

That inspired him. He couldn't remember anything he had learned, but he did have a shifter (which had sat unused for six months). So he decided to do shifting.

He shifted for a half hour a day, every day for one month — and improved his sight from 20/400 to 20/40. Photo by Sam Trotman on Unsplash.

He had access to the sun coming into his apartment from three directions, during a day, so he used his shifter eyes closed with the sun for a half hour a day, every day for one month.

By the end of that month, he was reading signs down on the street from way up high in his Manhattan apartment.

When he returned to his eye doctor, he discovered his vision had improved from 20/400 to 20/40. The doctor said, "Whatever you've been doing, keep doing it!"

VARIATION: USE THE SHIFTER IN CONJUNCTION WITH OTHER TECHNIQUES

One of the best results is obtained when the shifter is alternated with other techniques. For example, one of my students shifts for five minutes and then practices reading smaller type (where she has the most difficulty seeing clearly). Then she alternates: shifter, reading, shifter, reading — spending a few minutes on each one.

Interspersing the shifter into her practice with letters has been a huge success: Her glasses were +5.50 right eye and +6.50 left eye, but now she is able to read 4-point type with good light, and book-size type in regular light,

WHY BEGIN YOUR VISION IMPROVEMENT WITH A SHIFTER?

In 1984, an experience I had with an early client, Marilyn, made me take a hard look at my vision students.

Some were getting great results and improved steadily. Others improved extremely fast. But still others had little or no improvement.

As a new teacher, I took responsibility for that. Although I had been trained in hundreds of techniques, I didn't yet understand the importance of one over the other, or how they worked together.

Marilyn changed all that. She made me look at the importance of shifting to their recovery.

I was startled with what I discovered.

Just like in Marilyn's case, I found that my students who did not shift very well — or didn't bother to do it — had little or no improvement. This also applied to those who used a shifter but failed to see stationary objects moving (see Section 2 of this training).

Those who used a shifter daily and got interested in seeing stationary objects moving were improving at a steady, fast rate.

That woke me up.

With those students who had been getting very little improvement, I began focusing exclusively on shifting and swinging, until they could do them easily, and applied them daily.

Every single one of them began to see a dramatic improvement in their eyesight.

So I stopped trying to teach new students other techniques until they mastered shifting.

That didn't take very long. Within a few days they could move on to other techniques. That doesn't mean they stopped shifting. No. But the shifting and the sense of motion became second nature to them.

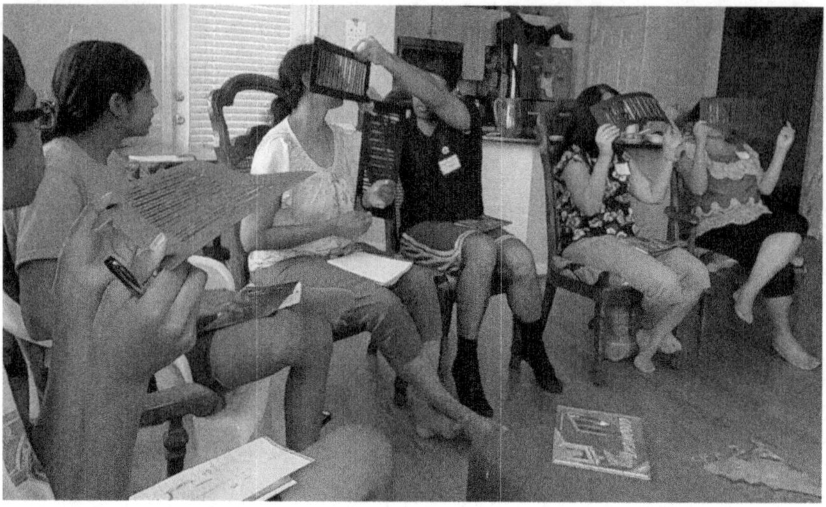

Students at one of Gloria's Super Sight Seminars, learning how to use a shifter. Shifting makes it possible to get results with other techniques.

Now I can usually move a student through shifting and swinging into central fixation or memory/imagination in one lesson (yes, one hour).

But I am not physically with you right now. You are doing this on your own. So take a little time with shifting (and with swinging, when we get to that next). Spend a week or two with it.

Let it seep into your psyche until you get that unconscious shifting of the eyes back again. Do this before you do anything else. And watch your vision improve.

Without shifting, you are wasting your time with other techniques.

MARILYN'S STORY: THE POWER OF SHIFTING

When I first began teaching this method in 1978, I did not understand the importance of shifting. Most of my students made steady improvement. Others, however, received little or no benefit, and I had no idea why.

Marilyn gave me the answer. She was nearsighted with a -4.50 prescription. That wasn't so unusual, but I quickly discovered her eyes did not shift. They made large movements, but no tiny, involuntary shifts. Even the sun shifter — which had never failed before — was not able to get her eyes shifting.

I was amazed and perplexed. After trying every other shifting technique I knew, I then began inventing them — to no avail. After awhile, we gave up and tried other types of techniques.

When I became an instructor I had learned over 500 techniques. Not knowing what else to do for Marilyn, we proceeded to go through each one.

For six months, we worked twice each week on her vision. I felt there had been no real progress, and questioned whether we should continue. But Marilyn wanted to keep going. Her reading vision had improved, and she had faith we would find a way through the stalemate. She had more faith than I did at that time; I was a new, inexperienced teacher.

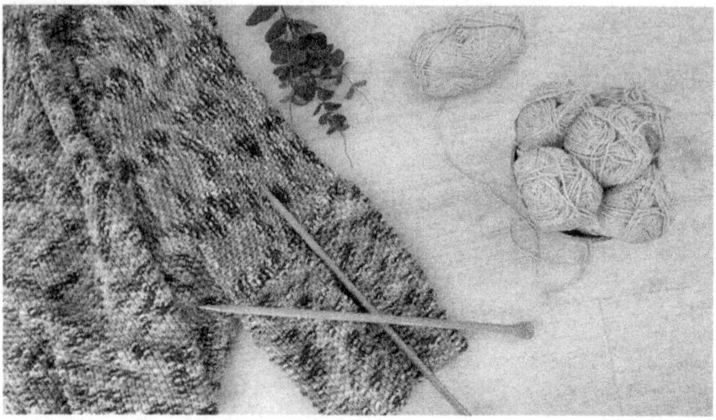

Desperate for results, I grabbed a knitting needle and had Marilyn run the rounded end across a shifter, like a mallet on a xylophone — and suddenly her eyes began shifting. After that, her vision improved. Photo by Les Triconautes on Unsplash

One day in a session with Marilyn, as I was demonstrating the concept of shifting, I picked up a knitting needle that was lying on the table, gave it to her, and asked her to move the rounded tip back and forth across a shifter.

Her hands could feel the shift as the needle thumped from slot to slot. Her ears could hear the clank-clank-clank sound which resulted from each shift.

Suddenly, her eyes began shifting.

We kept up the shift using the knitting needle for about 15 minutes. As she left, she went out through the anteroom in which my next student, Joel, was waiting for his lesson. Joel was palming and did not see Marilyn, but he recognized her voice.

After she left, Joel asked, "What happened with Marilyn today?"

"What do you mean?" I replied.

"Her voice," he explained. "It is completely different.

Before, it had a harsh quality, a sharp edge. But today, it was melodious. Something really changed with her today."

"Yes, we finally got her eyes to shift," I answered. But until he mentioned it, I hadn't noticed that the consequent relaxation was reflected in her voice.

After that, Marilyn's vision began to improve quickly. For a few weeks, she used a variation of the knitting needle-on-a-shifter technique. Then she graduated to shifting entirely visually.

When Marilyn's eyes began to shift, the strain left her nervous system — and even her voice became melodious. Drawing from Shutterstock.

SHIFTING WITHOUT A SHIFTER — HEAD SWING

The shifter gave you the feel of how the eyes shift with normal sight. It gets the natural shifting of the eyes and mind going again, which paves the way for shifting without a shifter.

When you use a shifter, you are doing a head swing. The next step is to remove the shifter and keep up the head swing.

THE ART OF READING

When reading, you should look at the white spaces between the lines, words or letters, and not directly at the lines themselves. The reason for this is that it is no effort to sweep the eyes over a plain background. Fixing the eyes on individual words and letters involves strain, and strain impairs vision.

When a person with normal sight regards the white spaces between the lines with a sweeping shift across the page, he can read easily, rapidly and without fatigue. If the same person looks at the letters, the eyes grow tired and the vision becomes poor.

People who cannot read well at the near point always tend to fix their attention on the print. Consequently, they see worse. Improvement cannot take place until they learn to look at the white spaces.

1. Turn a page of print turned on its side, and put it very close to your face — less than six inches (*see images*).
2. With eyes open, turn your head from left to right, just as you would do with a shifter — as if you were saying, "no, no" to a child.
3. Notice that the page will appear to move to the left when you move to the right, and vice versa. This motion is called a *swing*.

Because the eyes are light-finders, they shift across the black lines of text, seeking the white between the lines. The page works as a mini-shifter.

Turn the page on its side, bring it closer than six inches, shift the head and eyes from left to right. The lines of type work like a "mini-shifter."

TIPS FOR SUCCESS

- Bring the page so close that it almost touches your face.
- Don't focus or de-focus your eyes. Instead, let them move with your head.

HEAD SWING — STEP TWO

Now take the page down, keep up the head swing, and shift your gaze from side to side across the room from one side to the other.

Move easily, lazily and continuously, as if you had a shifter in front of you.

Once you have the experience of your eyes shifting unconsciously, you can shift all day long, every time you move your gaze from one point to another. Move the head to see, and allow the eyes to move as a result of the head motion.

See all all the points in between, as if there were a shifter connecting the points and you are gliding across all the slats on the shifter.

Turn the head from side to side while allowing your gaze to glide across the room — shifting without a shifter. Works best if you move extremely slowly.

TIPS FOR SUCCESS

- Allow the eyes to follow the head, so the head and eyes move in the same direction. This is true for all vision-improvement exercises.

- Never think about your eyes. Don't think of looking with your eyes. Don't hold them stationary, move them consciously or make an effort to see more clearly. Instead, place your attention ***gently*** on what you are seeing. The eyes focus where the attention is, so thinking of what you are seeing, rather than on what your eyes are doing, encourages the eyes to focus.
- To avoid the habit of looking with your eyes, imagine you are seeing from the back of the head, or that your nose is seeing. That is easier to do if you move your head or body to see.
- Move ***slowly***: Take six to eight seconds to move from left to right, and the same amount of time to move back to the left.

The head swing, long swing and sway CAN improve your eyesight — but only if you allow the eyes to move freely and unconsciously as a result of the head or body movement.

TURN THE WORLD INTO A SHIFTER: USE THE HEAD SWING OR SWAY ANYWHERE, ANYTIME

Practicing with the shifter can sharpen the vision and give you the feel of how to shift properly.

But you can't use a shifter all day long.

Children move their heads to see. This encourages a more rapid unconscious shift in the eyes Photo by Caroline Hernandez on Unsplash.

For lasting improvement in your eyesight, turn the world into a shifter. Move your head to see, so you eyes shift unconsciously. Whenever you look from one point to another, shift your gaze, and see all the points in between, just as if there were a shifter in front of you.

Watch a child, a dog or a cat, and you will see they always move their heads to see. The eyes move only as a result of the head movement. Photos: *Above* by *Pretty Fly For a Ty guy, Below* by *Jf Brou*, both on Unsplash

With imperfect sight, there is a tendency to stare at the first point, de-focus the eyes and then leap to the next point. Don't do that!

Instead, shift from one detail to another. See all the points in between, just as you would with a shifter. Don't skip points.

TROUBLESHOOTING: THE WRONG WAY TO SHIFT

It is possible to shift in a wrong way, strain your eyes and get no improvement. Following are wrong ways to shift:

- Imagining things stationary, or making an effort to stop the shifting. These make the vision become imperfect.
- Staring at a point without blinking or moving. This produces fatigue, distress or pain.
- When pain, fatigue or other symptoms are present it means there is a conscious or unconscious effort to see stationary objects stationary. The effort is a strain.
- "Jumping" from point to point. When the shifting becomes jerky, this is an indicator that you are not seeing all the points in between, and instead are staring consecutively at one point and then another. The vision will not improve.
- Seeing, or attempting to see, objects in the periphery better than those in the center of sight.

THE RIGHT WAY TO SHIFT

The right way to shift is to move the attention from one point to another slowly, regularly, continuously, restfully or easily, without effort or without trying to see.

Allow the eyes to move unconsciously with the attention.

CHAPTER 2

SEE STATIONARY OBJECTS MOVING

THE EASIEST WAY TO IMPROVE YOUR EYESIGHT

Objects that move with you (such as a bus) appear to be stationary while the stationary objects (buildings, roads, signs) appear to move. It REALLY helps vision to see this motion. Photo by Alex Smith on Unsplash.

With normal sight, stationary objects appear to be moving.This motion is called the ***swing***.

I know, I know. Stationary objects are not really moving. But that is the way they ***look***.

And vision is all about how things ***appear***, not about how things ***are***.

There are optical illusions of perfect sight, such as the swing, and there are optical illusions of imperfect sight, such as seeing a sign blurred when it is not blurred at all.

This is not the time or place to go into detail on the illusions of sight. (*That is an advanced training.*)

Suffice it to say, if you want to see with normal sight, you have to adopt the illusions of vision that the normal-sighted person has. One of these illusions is the illusion of stationary objects moving.

To see clearly, see stationary objects moving.

Even noticing moving objects moving can help your vision, because to see things moving requires the eyes to shift.

Consider a movie: It is composed of still picture frames, one after the other, 24 frames per second. This shift from one picture to another produces the illusion of motion.

The eye with normal sight shifts 70-100 times per second. This makes for an even smoother sense of motion.

If you see it.

Even seeing moving objects can help. Photo by *Justin Leibow* on *Unsplash.*

WHY DO YOU NEED TO SEE *STATIONARY* OBJECTS MOVE? WHY NOT JUST NOTICE MOVING OBJECTS?

Watching the movement of moving objects does coax your eyes to shift, which is a good thing.

But when you see stationary objects moving, your eyes must shift unconsciously. This is better, because there is no way you can consciously move your eyes 100 times per second all day long. It's not going to happen.

All people who get fast improvement in eyesight have one thing in common: They love seeing stationary objects moving. They observe it; they study it; they get excited about it. In essence, they "fall in love" with motion, and see it all day long.

Although you are the one moving, it ***looks*** *like the stationary objects are moving. You can see that here, with the motion of the buildings and trees.* Photo by *Dimon Bir* on *Unsplash.*

JOHN'S EXPERIENCE WITH MOTION

That's what happened with John. He was farsighted, and had worn glasses since he was four years old.

Every year, his vision had become worse, until by age 19 he was barely able to read the top letter on a test card — six inches high. And he could only do *that* if the test card was as close as three feet.

The smallest letters he could read close up at 12 inches were the size of front-page headlines on a newspaper — letters more than an inch in height — larger than 72 point.

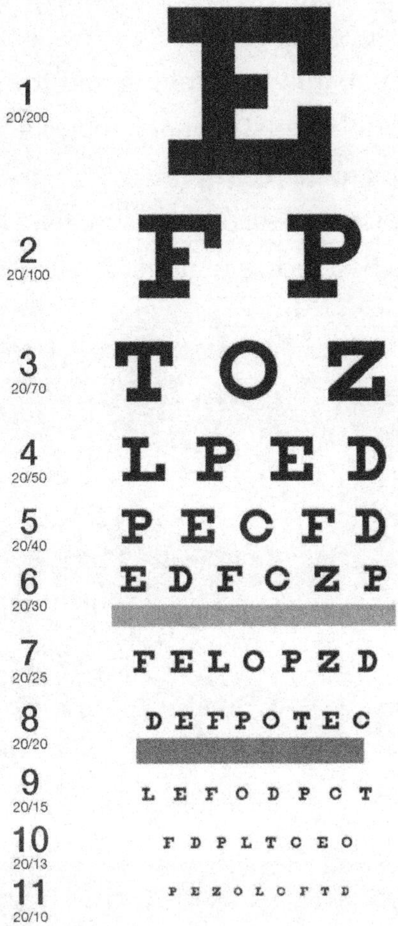

John could only read the top letter on a test card -- and he could only do that if it was as close as three feet.

John came to see me in August, one month before he began college. Because his vision was so poor, I thought he would need to practice several hours each day to improve it. Because he was starting college in a few weeks, that didn't seem feasible.

I suggested he take three or four lessons to learn how to

keep his sight from getting worse, and then come back in the summer to really fix his vision.

After sun shifting, palming, blinking and the long swing, I showed him how to see stationary objects moving. He "caught" the idea — and loved it!

When he came for his second lesson ten days later, he could to read letters two inches high at 15 feet!

Ten days later, he could read letters two inches high — 15 feet away. All from seeing stationary objects moving. Photo by Georgia de Lotz on *Unsplash.*

"What have you been practicing?" I asked.

"I use the shifter, and do the long swing, off and on," he replied, "And I palm a few times a day."

But mostly, I see things move. When I'm in a registration line at school, I sway and see things moving. When I walk, I see things moving. I just see things moving all day long."

John's experience is not an isolated case. Seeing stationary objects can transform your eyesight — and it's easy to do.

HOW TO START SEEING STATIONARY OBJECTS MOVING

Let's start with the easiest way to demonstrate the optical illusion of stationary objects moving: the Hand Swing.

TECHNIQUE #1: HAND SWING

Hand Swing: *Look past the hand and turn the head from left to right. The hand appears to move.*

1. Hold your hand about six inches in front of your face, with the palm facing in toward the face. Spread the fingers.
2. Keep the hand stationary.
3. With eyes open, look beyond the hand, across the room, and move your head from left to right as if you were using a shifter, or as if you were saying,

"no, no" to a child. Allow your eyes to move with your head but do not consciously move them.

4. Memory Swing: While turning the head, close the eyes and imagine the hand is moving opposite you. This motion may be even easier with eyes closed.
5. Alternate eyes open and closed: seeing the hand swing and then remembering the swing.

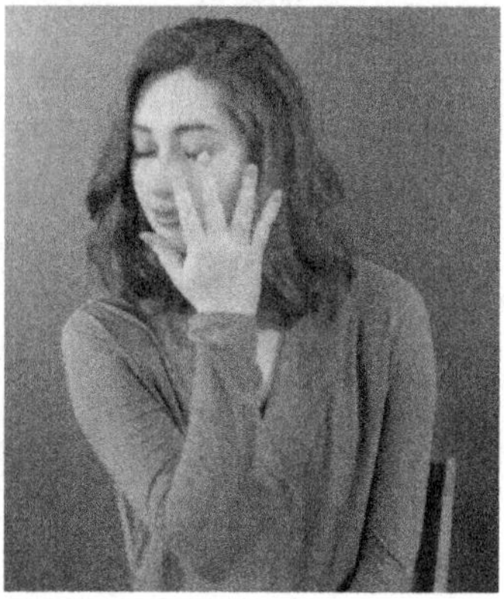

***Memory Swing**: While turning the head from left to right with eyes closed, imagine the hand swinging in the opposite direction.*

Does the hand appear to move?
If so, experiment by moving the hand slightly farther away. Then pick up an object — a phone, cup, piece of paper, pen. Hold it in your hand while you do the same technique. See the object appearing to move?

Set the object down on a table or desk (or any piece of furniture in front of you. Shift your gaze from one side to another of the object. See it moving? If not, put it a bit closer and look past it while you shift.

You can "swing" any object by shifting from one side of it to another and seeing the object move.

WHAT TO DO IF YOU DON'T SEE THE HAND MOVING

If you do not see the hand appearing to move, put the hand closer to your face — only a few inches away. Make sure you are not trying to focus on the hand itself. Look farther away, across the room, and look from one side of the room to the other with the hand in front of you.

LEARN HOW TO SEE MOTION — TECHNIQUE #2: HALLWAY SWING

1. Stand at one end of a hallway, or corridor — the narrower the better.
2. With the eyes closed, take two or three steps forward very rapidly.
3. While continuing to walk, open the eyes.
4. Alternate walking a few steps with your eyes closed and then open.

Hallway Swing: *Seeing motion in a hallway is easy. Take a few steps with the eyes closed, and then open them while you are walking. The walls, ceiling and floor will appear to move past you as you walk.* Photo by Lori Ayre on *Unsplash.*

Do the walls appear to move past you? This is especially obvious when your first open your eyes while walking. The ceiling also moves over your head and the floor moves under your feet.

WHAT TO DO IF YOU DON'T SEE THE HALLWAY MOVE

- Get a friend to walk right beside you, touching your arm or shoulder so you can relax knowing you will not bump into a wall.
- Walk much faster — run if you can, for a few steps.
- See from the back of the head (described in Chapter 4 of this book).

LEARN HOW TO SEE MOTION — TECHNIQUE #3: THE SWAY

The sway not only helps you to see the motion, it also allows you to continue to see it all day long. The easiest way to demonstrate this is standing in front of a window.

***Sway**: Stand facing a window and sway the body from side to side. The window appears to move.* Photo by Peter Kisteman on Unsplash

Here's how to do it:

1. Stand facing a window, less than an arm's length away, and put yourself close to the side so you can see the window frame.

2. Sway the body from side to side while looking outside the window.
3. As you sway, the window appears to move slightly from side to side, with a short swinging motion.
4. The window moves in the opposite direction from you, while outside the window, the farthest objects appear to move in the same direction as you.
5. You can also sway while sitting.
6. If you don't see the window swinging, stand closer to it, make a wider sway, or do 100 long swings first.

If you don't see the motion, get closer to the window. Photo by Anaya Katlego on Unsplash

Does the window appear to move? The window and the window frame will appear to move in the opposite direction from you.

HERE'S WHAT TO DO NEXT:

- **Step farther away from the window**: Gradually move farther away and continue to see the window swinging.
- **Shorten the sway**: Gradually, you can reduce the width of the sway, so you can see the window swing with just a very tiny sway from side to side.
- **Practice with other objects**: Sway and see objects on a table swinging, or items in a store, furniture in a room, or trees, signs and buildings swinging as you sway.

Sway anywhere, anytime — and see stationary objects moving. Photo by Lê Tân on Unsplash

LEARN HOW TO SEE MOTION — TECHNIQUE #4: LONG SWING

When it is difficult to see stationary objects moving, the long swing can break through the block. It works directly on the cerebral-spinal nervous system to stimulate the unconscious shifting of the eyes.

This makes it much easier for you to see stationary objects moving.

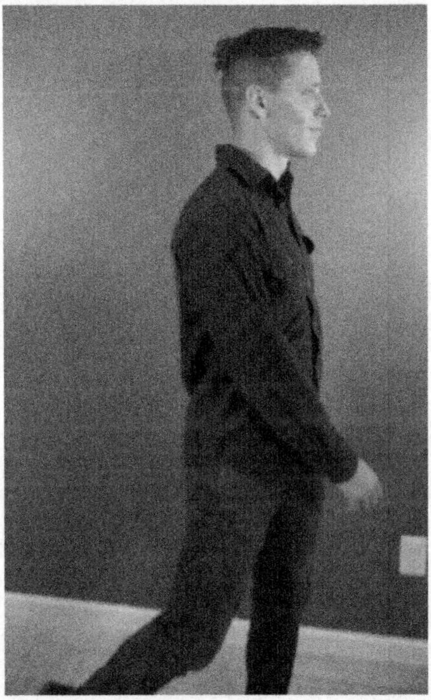

Do 100 Long Swings every night before sleep, or anytime you want to turn on your sense of stationary objects moving.

Doing 100 long swings before you go to bed at night sends you to sleep with your eyes shifting instead of staring — so you wake up with better vision. One hundred swings takes about three minutes, or the length of one song.

> "The long swing not only improves the vision, but also relieves pain, discomfort and fatigue."
>
> *WILLIAM H. BATES, MD*

HERE'S HOW TO DO IT:

1. Stand facing one wall with your feet about one foot apart. Sway the body from side to side, shifting the weight from one foot to the other while keeping the spine straight.
2. To turn the sway into a long swing, lift the left heel a short distance from the floor while turning the body toward the right until the shoulders, hips, head and eyes are parallel with the wall. Keep the back straight from the base of the spine to the top of the head.
3. Then turn the body to the left, lifting the heel of the right foot a few inches from the floor.
4. Alternate swinging left and right.

TIPS FOR SUCCESS

- Do not turn the head on the shoulders or move the eyes in the head. The movement is initiated by turning from the hip, not from the waist.

- Swing easily, continuously, without effort and without paying any attention to the apparent movement of objects in front of you.

WHEN TO PRACTICE THE LONG SWING

Before you go to sleep every night, do 100 long swings (about three minutes). You can also do the long swing anytime to refresh your sense of motion.

MOTION GETS YOUR *MIND* SHIFTING

When you see stationary objects moving, it is not just the eyes that are shifting, it is the **mind** that is shifting.

In order to see the swing, you have to leave one point behind, mentally, and shift to another point.

Because the sense of motion not only releases the visual stare, but also the mental stare, it makes a permanent improvement in the eyesight.

So stop staring. Instead, shift and swing: See stationary object moving.

IMPROVE YOUR VISION ANYWHERE, ANYTIME, DOING ANYTHING — BY SEEING STATIONARY OBJECTS MOVING

Right now, it will be easiest for you to see motion when you are moving yourself. So start there. See the apparent motion of stationary objects whenever you walk, ride a bike, drive a car, reach for something, or move in any way.

When driving, see the road moving under the car, and the trees and buildings to the side moving past you. Photo by Jaromír Kavan on Unsplash

- ***Driving***: See the buildings, trees and other scenery moving past you, the road moving under the car, and freeway signs moving over your head.

Move the head to read, and see the background behind the page moving with you, while the book moves opposite you. Photo by Thought Catalog on Unsplash.

- ***Reading***: The book appears to move opposite you while the background beyond the book moves with you.

When you walk, see the ground move under your feet, and the scenery to the side moving past you. Photo by Henry Xu on Unsplash.

- ***Walking***: Notice the trees, buildings, parked cars, etc. moving past you while the ground appears to move under your feet. Walking indoors, see the furniture, floor, ceiling and walls moving past you.

Sway to see the screen moving. Whenever you are sitting in one place for a period of time, the sway will give you a way to continue to see motion. Photo by Chris Montgomery on Unsplash

- ***When sitting or looking at a computer***: Sway to produce the illusion of stationary objects swinging. Even the smallest sway can sharpen the vision.
- ***Notice the difference in motion at different distances***: The farthest objects, such as clouds, hills, moon or sun appear to move in the the same direction as you do, as if they were following you.

Close objects move wider and faster than farther objects. Observing the different degrees of motion helps vision greatly. Photo by Stephen G. on Unsplash

Whenever the head and eyes move, see stationary objects moving relative to your movement. Every time you move your attention from one detail to another, shift from point to point and see the relative motion, the swing, which results.

> ***It doesn't take any time out of your day to see stationary objects moving — and it can transform your vision.***

With conscious practice, shifting and swinging become second nature, and you'll find yourself doing them unconsciously all day long.

HOW TO KEEP UP THE MOTION WHEN YOU ARE NOT MOVING YOURSELF

With normal sight, the sense of stationary objects moving extends to looking at a stationary point without moving the head, eyes or body.

For example, when looking at a period on a page of print, the period appears to swing slightly, with a pendulum-like motion.

This is called the ***Optical Swing*** of the normal eye. It occurs because with normal sight the eye and mind are constantly shifting, producing the illusion that stationary objects constantly appear to move.

The Optical Swing is the final goal of motion. The shifter, long swing, head swing, sway and other motion techniques all lead to the optical swing, and finally to the Universal Swing.

These are way too advanced to go into here. But it may help you to know what the goal of all this shifting and swinging is:

Never see a stationary object stationary

HERE'S WHAT STUDENTS SAY ABOUT MOTION AND VISION

"The first technique Gloria talked about was motion. People can't see when they stare. When people stare, their eyes are not moving enough. The camera is not taking enough pictures. Without enough pictures, there is not enough resolution, and the picture is blurry.

"First, you have to get motion going. If you move to the left, things appear to move to the right. Let them move.

". . . I went outside and walked along the wall of the parking lot. I thought about the fact that the wall had to move in the opposite direction from me, and that I had to let it move.

"As I stayed aware of the wall's apparent motion, I felt as if I would fall. Then I felt seasick. After a while, I went back inside and looked at Gloria. Her face was no longer blurry."

ANN S.

There is something almost magical which happens by seeing stationary objects moving. Colors are brighter. The world becomes alive and three-dimensional:

"Learning to see the world move again brings back a sense of reality I had lost. It's more than just improving eyesight, it's relearning how to see!"

ROBERT M.

CHAPTER 3

USE A TEST CARD TO DISCOVER YOUR BEST TECHNIQUES

THE FASTEST WAY TO IMPROVE YOUR EYESIGHT

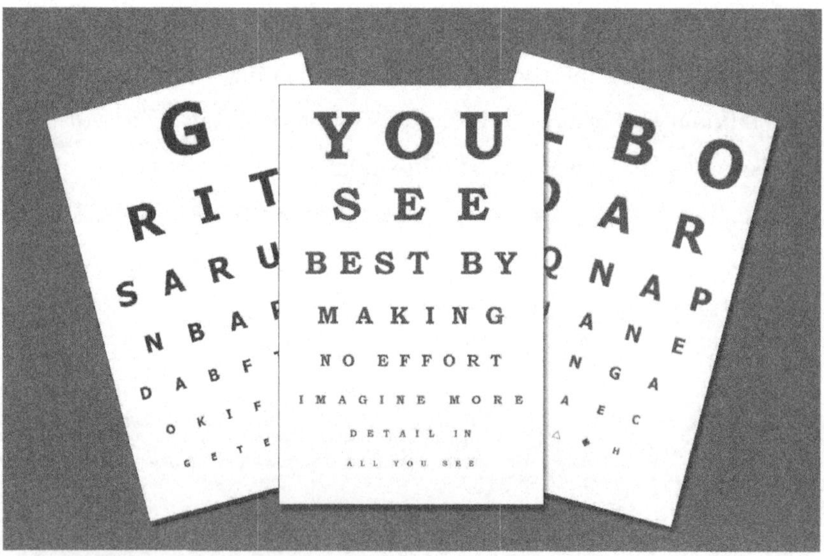

Letter-practice cards for your use are included at the back of this book

Using a letter-card with different sizes of letters is the fastest way to find out which techniques improve your eyesight — and also which ones don't work for you.

Vision is nine-tenths mental. People's minds are different. There is no way to know how ***YOU*** will respond to a specific technique without trying it out.

Fortunately, that is easy to do.

Vision techniques fall into three categories, the three Habits of the Normal Eye:

1. Motion
2. Effortless Focus
3. Mental Pictures

Some techniques overlap these categories. All have shifting and swinging as their basis.

DON'T WASTE TIME ON TECHNIQUES THAT DON'T WORK

When one technique works much better than another, you know where to start. Use the technique that sharpens your vision most often, and to the highest degree

Y O U

S E E

B E S T B Y

M A K I N G

N O E F F O R T

I M A G I N E M O R E

D E T A I L I N

A L L Y O U S E E

S E E M O T I O N A L L D A Y L O N G

Letters give you the best feedback as to what improves your vision. You can then apply your best techniques throughout the day, on other objects.

Here are four different approaches you can experiment with. One of them may give you much more improvement than another. That is the one to use.

How do you know if the technique worked for you? That's easy: You'll get a flash of improved vision. It won't last long at first — just a split second. That's okay. We'll build stamina later. Right now the objective is to be able to produce flashes of clarity. This clarity is your clue you are moving in the right direction.

If none of these techniques sharpens your vision, that may be because you do not fully understand how to apply it, or because that approach isn't the most direct one for you.

In either case, don't bother with the one(s) that don't improve your eyesight right now. Use the one(s) that do.

I know this sounds obvious, but most people don't do it. They will put a test card 20 feet away where they can barely see the top line, and then struggle to make the letters clear up.

If you do that, you are truly wasting your time.

USE FAVORABLE CONDITIONS

Work with the distance that is most favorable for you, the distance at which you can see the most frequent flashes of clarity in your vision.

Also: work with the type of technique that gives you the best results. Discard the one(s) that don't work so well.

After all, you don't need ten techniques. You just need one that works really well for you. Discovering which of the techniques gives you the most improvement helps define the approach which will give you perfect sight.

When you find that technique, practice it a lot. If it improves your vision with letters, it will also work with other objects. The more often you sharpen up your vision, the more quickly the clarity will become second-nature for you.

HOW TO FIND YOUR BEST TECHNIQUE(S)

The following instructions apply to all techniques

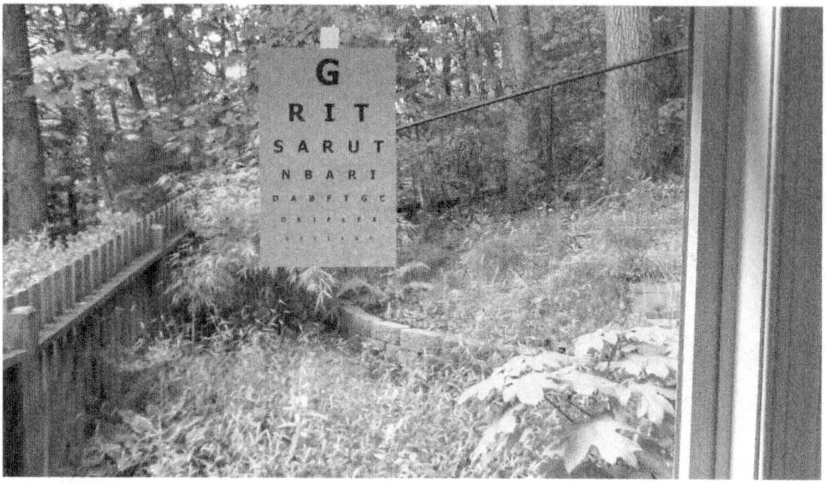

Tape a letter-card to a window. This makes it much easier to see the swing, and to do all the techniques.

1. Make a copy of one of the charts included with this book. Put the chart on a window (*see image*).
2. Take off your glasses (or contact lenses, if you wear them).
3. Use a shifter or do long swings for 3-5 minutes to loosen up and get the sense of motion going. ***DO NOT SKIP THIS STEP***. Why? Because if you do, you most likely will not get results from the techniques. And you want your vision to improve, right?

After shifting, stand close enough to the chart that you can read everything except the last two lines. This may be two feet or ten feet away, depending on your vision.

Read down as far as you can without strain. You'll see better results if you are close enough that you can read the second or third line from the bottom.

Start at the top. Read one letter at a time. Go as far down the card as you can without strain, with both eyes together and each eye separately.

BEGIN WITH TWO EYES TOGETHER

Start with both eyes. When you see more clearly while doing the technique, do the same technique with each eye separately.

Be sure when you use one eye that the distance of the chart is close enough that the eye can read everything except the bottom line.

You may have to be 18 inches away from the chart with one eye while you can be five or six feet away with the other.

You may find one eye responds differently than the other. For example, the left eye may get great results with the memory swing but not with the technique of seeing the periphery worse — while the right eye may be exactly the opposite.

When practicing with one eye, cover the other eye with the palm of the hand. Do not put pressure on the eyeball. Do not close the eye that is covered. Both eyes open and close ***together*** at all times, whether one eye is covered or not.

Now, try out four different techniques, to see which approach gives you the most improvement in your vision.

TEST CARD TECHNIQUE #1: SHIFTING AND SWINGING

Here's how to do it:

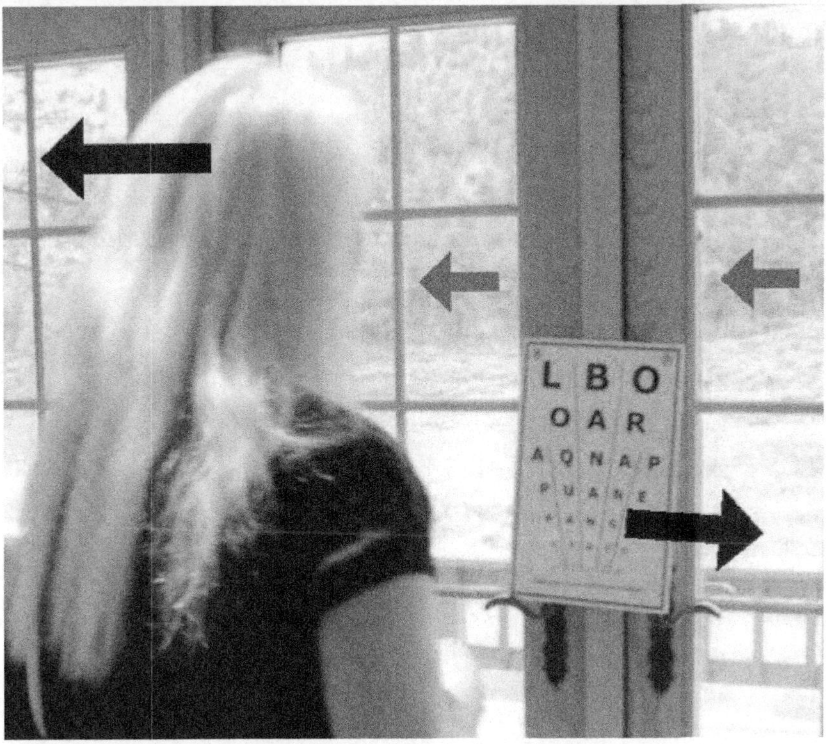

When you sway to the left, the background outside the window also moves to the left, while the letter-card and the window appear to move to the right.

1. Sway or do a head swing while shifting your gaze left and right across the last line of letters you can read easily. When you sway to the left, glide the gaze to the left. When you sway to the right, glide the gaze to the right.
2. Notice that the chart appears to move in the opposite direction: When you move to the right, the chart (and window) appears to move to the left, and vice versa.
3. Objects outside the window appear to move in the same direction as you do.

Focus on the motion — not the clarity.

TIPS FOR SUCCESS

- Keep your peripheral vision open: See the entire field of vision.
- Keep swaying or doing a head swing, and see the motion of the chart against the background.
- Look outside for a few swings while you continue swaying, and see the chart moving in your peripheral vision, Then shift across the letters again, and see the background move. (Keep swaying!)
- Alternate seeing the swing while looking close and far.

Swing road signs when you are stopped at a light. Photo by Brendan Church on Unsplash.

PRACTICE SHIFTING AND SWINGING WITHOUT LETTERS — ANYWHERE, ANYTIME

Do the letters seem clearer? If so, apply the same technique to other objects. For example, in your car when stopped at a traffic light, sway slightly and see the windshield move relative to the background, or a road sign move relative to a building.

TEST CARD TECHNIQUE #2: MEMORY SWING

Here's how to do it:

1. With the letter-card at a distance where you can read all but the last line, sway or do a head swing while shifting across a line of letters you can read. Notice the card moves opposite you while the background moves with you.
2. Close your eyes and remember the swing, while continuing to sway. When you move to the left, the letters move to the right. When you move to the right, they move to the left.
3. Open the eyes and see the card move, then close the eyes and imagine it moving. Alternate seeing the swing and remembering it.

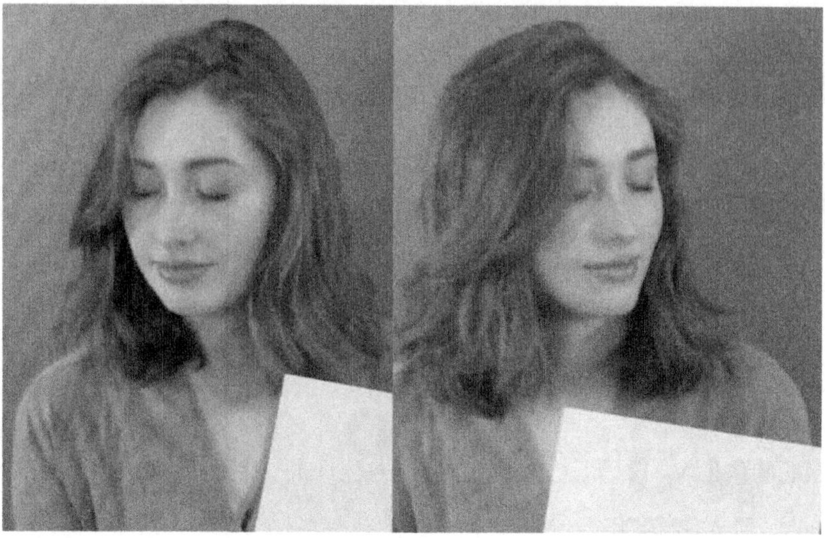

***Memory Swing:** Turn the head from side to side, and see the letter-card move opposite you. Then close your eyes, keep up the head swing, and remember the card swinging. Alternate eyes open and closed.*

Do you find when you first open your eyes that the letters appear clearer for a moment? That is because the memory of motion relaxed the strain, and you were still in that state of mind of relaxation when you first opened your eyes.

TIPS FOR SUCCESS

The key to success with this technique is to put your attention on the memory or imagination of the swing, rather than on how clear the letters are.

Focus on the memory — not the clarity.

PRACTICING WITHOUT LETTERS — ANYWHERE, ANYTIME

If the memory swing helps you see better, spend a few minutes a day practicing it with letters, and then apply it throughout the day.

Take a few seconds' break from your computer to sharpen up your vision: Sway slightly from side to side. See the edge of the screen move relative to the background (a wall or window behind it).

Close your eyes and remember the swing. Open your eyes and see the swing. Alternate two or three times.

Is your computer screen clearer now?

You can imagine a memory swing anywhere, any time you can safely close your eyes for a few seconds. Swing the edge of your car windshield, or a sign at a checkout counter in a store. Any vertical line will work.

When you can't close your eyes, you can draw an infinity sign in your mind, over and over. This is a way of carrying the swing with you wherever you are.

Imagine an infinity sign, and trace its shape continuously — in the mind. The eyes will shift unconsciously when you do.

TEST CARD TECHNIQUE #3: SEEING THE PERIPHERY WORSE

Here's how to do it:

1. Sway or do a head swing while shifting across a line of letters, and notice the movement of the card against the background.
2. Look a few inches below (or above, or to the side of) the letters to a nondescript, blank surface, such as a wall, field of grass, carpet, or sky. Keep swaying or doing the head swing.
3. Notice the letters look worse in your peripheral vision, and the chart is moving.
4. Look back at the chart and shift across the letters again. Are they clearer than before?

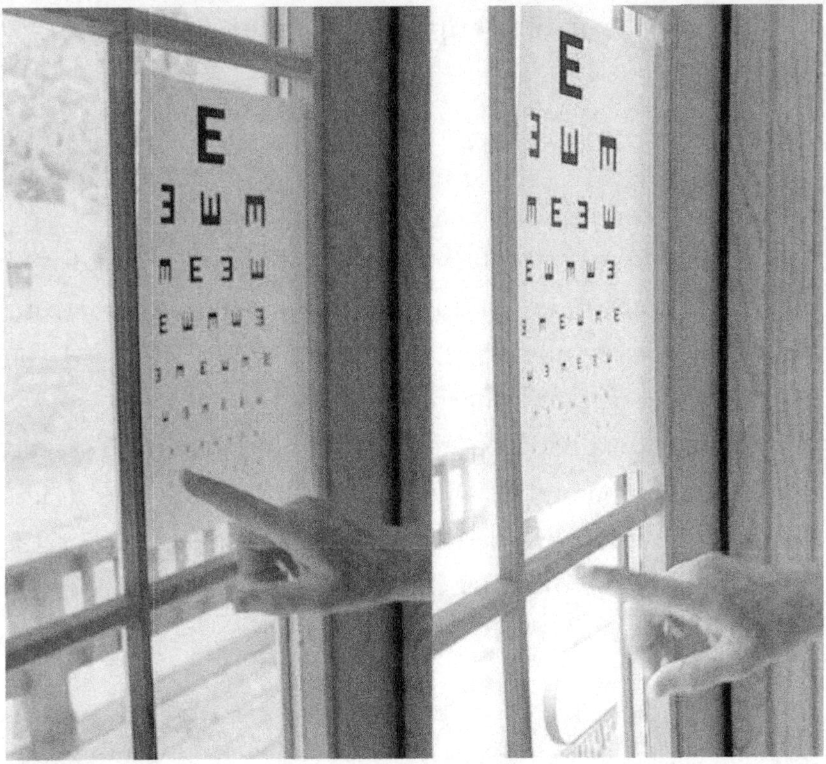

See the Periphery Worse: First, shift across the letters themselves, seeing the swing. Then look below the letters outside, while shifting from left to right under the chart. See the letters worse in the periphery. Then shift across the letters again.

TIPS FOR SUCCESS

- Look only as far away as necessary to see the letters worse in the periphery. You should still be able to see the letters in the periphery, but not be able to read them. If you look too far away, this technique won't work.
- Put your attention on the letters looking worse in the periphery, and the motion of the card.

Focus on the periphery — not the detail.

PRACTICE WITHOUT LETTERS — ANYWHERE, ANYTIME

This is one of the easiest techniques to apply throughout your day. It is almost as simple to do as shifting or seeing stationary objects moving.

And it can instantly sharpen your vision.

Pick any detail: a face, cup, plant, objects on a desk, etc. Look just far enough away from the detail to see it less distinctly in the peripheral vision. Then look back at the detail again. When you let it look worse in the periphery, it often looks sharper when you come back to it.

See the Periphery Worse: *Look at a face. Then look away from the face to a mostly blank surface such as a wall, and see the face worse in the periphery. Look back at the face; see it better.* Photo by jhudel baguio on Unsplash

HOW SEEING THE PERIPHERY WORSE HELPS YOUR VISION IMPROVE

How does seeing the periphery worse make the detail better? Because your eyes focus where your mind is focused: When you look without effort, you see clearly. When you look at a blank surface, there is no effort to see.

When you notice how a detail is less distinct in the periphery, you are making no effort to see it. You are looking without effort — at a distance where ordinarily you would tend to strain (this is obvious, because if you have imperfect sight at that distance, you are straining).

You are in the state of mind necessary for perfect sight: looking without effort. For a moment when you look back at the detail, you are still in that state of mind, and therefore see the detail sharper.

The clarity, as with all of these techniques at this stage of your vision improvement, may only last for a second — a flash. That's because you inadvertently snap back into your habit of straining to see.

WHAT FLASHES DO FOR YOU

Every time you produce a flash of clarity, you are demonstrating to the mind how to see. The mind learns from experience — it needs to experience better vision to change its habit of strain. Every flash moves you closer to your goal of perfect sight.

This is a beginning book, so the goal right now is to produce clarity, in flashes. Later you will learn how to gain more control over your improving eyesight, so you can produce better vision on demand. And later still you will find the clarity coming in at other times when you are not practicing. Also, your baseline vision will rise, so that you are generally seeing better.

There are more stages beyond that, where improved eyesight becomes the norm for you, and where you have perfect sight continuously.

But for now, focus on producing flashes of clarity by changing how you are focusing your mind. Discover what helps you eliminate the mental effort to see — if only for a fraction of a second at a time.

TEST CARD TECHNIQUE #4: MEMORY OF DETAIL

Here's how to do it:

1. Sway or do a head swing while shifting across the last line of letters you can read easily.
2. Pick a letter from the smallest line you can read. Close your eyes and remember it. Recall its blackness. Trace the shape in your mind. This will give you a good mental picture of it.
3. Then — while still imagining the letter in your mind — open your eyes and shift across it again. If successful, the letters will appear clearer.

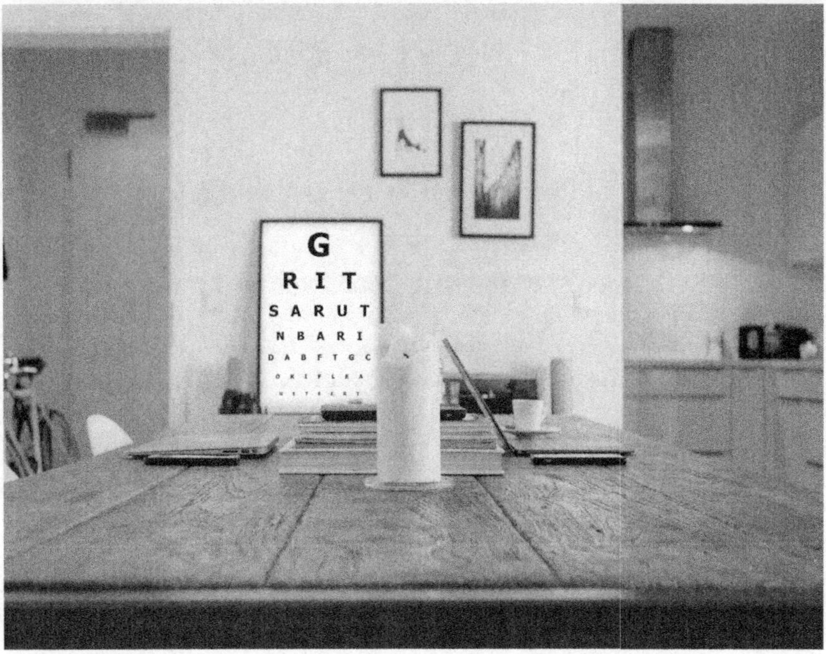

Memory of Detail: *Pick a letter. Close your eyes and remember it. Imagine it clearly. Open your eyes and see the next letter. Repeat.*Photo by Crew on Unsplash.

TIPS FOR SUCCESS

- If you can't imagine mental pictures, close your eyes and rest them, or palm. Open your eyes and look again. The letter will be clearer. Pick another letter. Repeat.
- If you stare, the letters will blur. Shift to break the stare. After you see each letter, quickly close your eyes and remember it. Then open your eyes and shift to another letter on the line.
- As your vision improves, practice with the smaller letters on the next lines.

ALTERNATE TECHNIQUE: MEMORY OF DETAIL CLOSE AND FAR

1. Use two of the same letter-cards. Hold one close enough to see it perfectly.
2. See the clear letter, close your eyes and remember it.
3. Keep remembering the clear letter when you open your eyes and look at the same letter farther away.

***Memory of Detail Close and Far**: Put charts at different distances. Remember a clear letter when looking at the same letter farther away,* Photo by Behzad Ghaffarian on Unsplash.

TIPS FOR SUCCESS

- Do not try to see the farther letter Instead, just ***remember the clear letter*** while looking farther.
- This is an advanced technique, so if you do not get results with it, don't worry. Use another technique for now, and this may work for you later.

The key to using a memory technique is:

Focus on the mental picture — not the vision.

HOW TO APPLY MEMORY OF DETAIL MOMENT-TO-MOMENT

If the memory of a detail improves your vision, you can apply this technique throughout the day in two ways:

1. Pick any detail in your environment, such as a letter or an icon on your phone, remember it with your eyes closed, and then open the eyes and remember the image while you are looking farther away.

1. **Eyes Open Memory**: Imagine a clear letter (or any other detail) in your mind while you are doing other activities: while you drive, eat a meal, or walk.

When used in this way, the mental picture is called a *Foundation Object*, because it provides you with the foundation for maintaining the state of mind of perfect sight. To remember or imagine something clearly, the eyes have to focus as if they would when seeing clearly.

PART TWO
FOUR KEYS TO SUCCESS
IT'S NOT WHAT YOU DO, BUT HOW YOU DO IT THAT'S IMPORTANT

It's not so much **what** *you do, as* **how** *you do it that's important. These four keys can make the difference between mediocre results and outstanding success.*
Photo by Jude Beck on Unsplash

CHAPTER 4

KEY #1: MAKE NO EFFORT TO SEE

IT'S NOT WHAT YOU DO, BUT HOW YOU DO IT

"The object of all the methods used in the treatment of imperfect sight without glasses is to secure rest or relaxation — of the mind first, and then of the eyes."

WILLIAM H. BATES, MD

One of my vision students, Anne, was visiting a mountain town with her 20-year-old daughter, who not only had perfect sight, but better than normal sight — 20/10 vision.

Anne was attempting to read a sign above a shop about a block away. But try as she might, she could not read those letters. So she asked her perfect-sighted daughter: "Cathy, can you read that sign over there — the yellow one with the red letters?"

Cathy took one look at the sign. "No," she said, and

promptly looked away. Anne was astonished. "She didn't even *try* to see it!" she exclaimed.

"She didn't even try to see it!" my student exclaimed. Her daughter had just demonstrated a fundamental principle about vision: With perfect sight, there is never an effort to see. Photo by Krista Joy Montgomery on Unsplash.

She was amazed because her daughter's response was so utterly different than her own. The experience made it clear what I had been teaching her for months: A person with normal sight never tries to see.

Now you might be thinking, "Of course the girl didn't try. She has perfect sight, Why would she try to see? Actually, it's the other way around. The reason she has perfect sight was because she doesn't try to see, even when pressured.

No matter how good your vision is, there will always be objects beyond your range of sight: objects too dim, too small, or too far away. But people with normal sight never try to see. They either see it, or they don't. End of story.

There will always be objects beyond your range of sight. But the person with normal sight never tries to see them. Photo by Bruce W on Unsplash.

Did it help my student to make an effort to see? No. She had been trying for awhile to read that sign. All she accomplished was to create frustration and lower her vision.

ANY EFFORT TO SEE LOWERS THE VISION

Any effort — whether conscious or unconscious — lowers vision. This effort undermines the effectiveness of any vision improvement technique: It is not so much *what* you do, but *how* you do it.

Do you strain to see when you are on a computer — like this woman is doing? The cause of this strain is the mistaken belief that to focus you need to make an effort. This is not true. Strain prevents you from focusing. Photo by Vadim Danilov on Unsplash.

Vision is never perfect when there is an effort to see. Perfect sight comes effortlessly, and in no other way.

With normal sight, vision is unconscious; it "just happens." When the sight is imperfect, there is a belief, whether conscious or unconscious, that focusing requires effort. This thought — all by itself — is enough to blur the vision.

It doesn't stop there. The effort is compounded by all the erroneous ideas we have about how the mind and eyes focus: We stare and try to concentrate, in the mistaken belief that we would focus better if we could exclude the peripheral vision and hold the mind and eyes on one point continuously.

We sincerely believe that to see, understand or "grasp" an idea we must make an effort. We fear if we don't "do" something, we won't succeed. And that very fear leads to failure.

You only need to look at a hunter when she is focused on her prey: There is absolutely no effort and absolutely total focus. Attention - Effort = Focus. Photo by Mike Marrah on Unsplash.

It is this wrong thought that causes the mental effort to see, the effort that blurs the vision. The truth is just the opposite: Focusing is easy and requires no effort.

Maximum focus occurs from zero effort.

> "The cause of [imperfect sight] is simply a thought — a wrong thought — and the cure is as quick as the thought that relaxes."

NEVER SQUINT, STARE OR STRAIN

You may get snatches of sharper vision when you use trick vision, such as squinting your eyelids partly closed. However, this will never bring your eyesight to normal, and if you keep it up your eyesight will continue to get worse.

Staring blurs the vision. The clarity drops in proportion to the length of time you stare. It is not possible to hold the mind or eyes on one point continuously. They can only focus on one point for a fraction of a second without shifting.

Replace the stare with shifting.

Don't try to clear up the blur. Focus on what you DO see. Photo by Alaric Duan on Unsplash.

IGNORE THE BLUR — DON'T TRY TO CLEAR THINGS UP

Never try to clear up the blur. Forget about it. Ignore it. Instead of fighting it, think of the blur as an opportunity to improve your vision.

What? It's simple: If you never look at anything blurred, you have no opportunity to improve. There is simply no room for improvement. You have to stretch your vision to go beyond where you are now.

Instead of trying to make letters or objects clearer, allow your eyes to be passive receivers of light. Think of the word *focus* as a passive verb instead of an active one: "Things are seen," not "I am seeing."

Relaxation of both the eyes and mind is necessary to see clearly, because it is the mental effort to see that causes the eyes to stare and strain. The eyes always follow the mind.

FOCUS ON WHAT YOU DO SEE

Imagine you are an impressionist artist and can see the world in a way no one else can. Notice what you see (color, shape and/or motion), without trying to change it. This clears up the vision. How? Because the eyes focus where the attention is.

Pretend you are an Impressionist artist, and can see the world in a way no one else can. Begin to observe what you see. Photo by Jessi Pena on Unsplash

VISION IS CHANGEABLE

Normal sight is not normal all the time; imperfect sight is not imperfect all the time. It all depends on the level of mental relaxation (or strain) that is present at any given moment.

CHAPTER 5
KEY #2 SEE FROM THE BACK OF THE HEAD

When there is no effort to see, it feels as though you are seeing from the back of the head. Photo by Hatham on Unsplash

When there is an effort to see, the attention is pushed forward toward the front of the face, as if we could think with our eyes.

But the eyes can't think. They can only receive light and pass that sensation to the brain. The mental strain to see causes the eyes to stare and the vision to blur.

You can eliminate this strain, and focus by putting yourself in the back of the head, opening up the peripheral vision, and allowing the eyes to shift

When there is no effort to see, when the sight is normal, it feels as though you have no eyes, that you are seeing from the back of the head.

You may more easily be able to let go of effort if you consciously imitate this sensation, and see from the back of the head. This widens the periphery, eliminates strain and improves vision.

Notice how in the picture above, this man is staring. His attention is pushed forward toward the front of the face, his field of vision narrowed. In the second photo (below), the man is seeing from the back of the head. Even the posture is different. Photos by Miguelangel Miquelena on Unsplash.

I once suggested to an accountant that he put himself in the back of the head instead of reaching out and trying to see. He replied, "How can I 'put' myself somewhere?" He didn't understand it, but began thinking about the concept.

A few weeks later, he woke up and found himself seeing from the back of the head. At his lesson that day, he said he had been "in the back of the head" all day — and was able to read print smaller than he had ever read before: tiny, one-point microprint.

He read for an entire hour, easily, rapidly and continuously — all because he had learned to see from the back of the head.

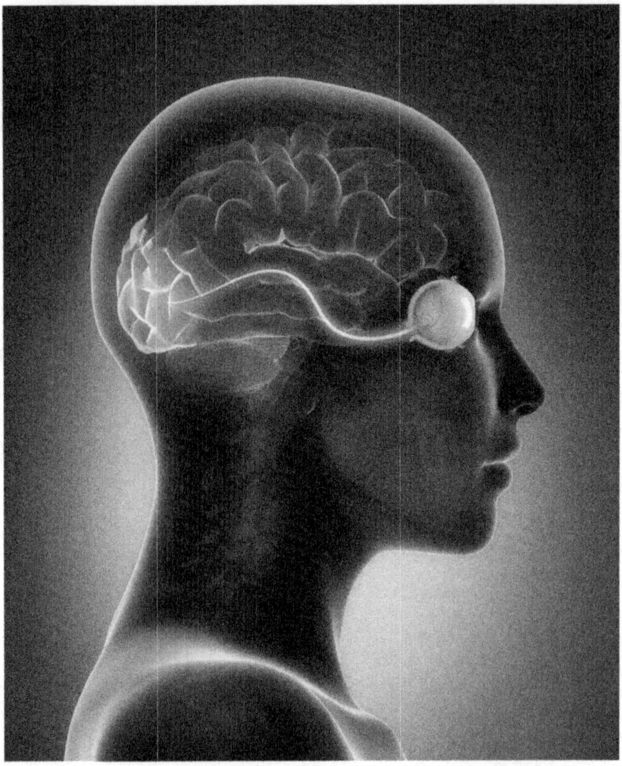

Sensory nerves are a "one way street." The eyes register light, and send the information to the brain. Any effort to see interferes with this process. Illustration from Shutterstock.

The retinal nerves are sensory nerves. They receive impressions from the outside world, and send those sensations to the brain for processing. These nerves are passive receptors of sensation, "one-way streets" that go only one direction: toward the brain.

Each of the five senses works in this way. Nerves of taste, touch, smell and hearing receive sensation and send it to the brain.

The Visual Cortex is in the back of the head. This is where the pictures you see are created. Light rays come into the eyes, and the sensation travels through the optic nerves and enters the brain in the back of the head.

Light comes through the eyes effortlessly, just as music comes to the ears. With normal hearing, you are unaware of your ears. For normal sight, be just as unaware of your eyes: See from the back of the head.

To see with normal sight, you need to use your eyes the way normal-sighted people do: See from the back of the head — and open up your field of vision.

CHAPTER 6

KEY #3 OPEN UP YOUR PERIPHERAL VISION

To see clearly, use your entire field of vision. Open up your peripheral vision!
Photo by Samuel Clara on Unsplash.

"Concentrate!" Have you ever heard that? It is a mistaken belief that you focus best when you block out the periphery. This idea has caused more myopia than any other concept.

Concentration, trying to focus on one thing only, doesn't work. It is a strain, and lowers the vision.You do not focus by seeing one thing only. You focus by seeing one thing best and everything else peripherally.

Strain narrows the field of vision and causes a blur. Photo by Grzegorz Walczak on Unsplash.

Don't block out the periphery. Never concentrate, or narrow your gaze. Focus by seeing both the detail and the periphery.

You can only see detail clearly when you see it as part of a whole picture. To see clearly, use the entire field of vision.

WHEN TO PRACTICE SEEING THE PERIPHERY

Not only when you are practicing with letters, but also at all other times, see the periphery around things. This eliminates the effort of trying to see detail, and encourages sharper focus.

When using a phone, see the periphery around it, like the man in this photo is doing. Photo by Qim Manifester on Unsplash.

- When using a phone, keep your peripheral vision open.
- When looking at a face, see the background around the person.
- When watching television or using a computer, see the periphery outside the screen. The wider the periphery, the sharper the vision.

When reading or writing, see the periphery outside the page.
Photo by Hannah Olinger on Unsplash.

- When reading or writing, see the periphery outside the page.

CHAPTER 7
KEY #4 STOP USING GLASSES
OR REDUCE YOUR PRESCRIPTION, AND USE THEM AS SELDOM AS POSSIBLE

You cannot make any lasting improvement in your vision if you continue to use full-strength glasses. Photo by Yi ZhU on Unsplash

"It is a mistake to believe that even though glasses do no good they cannot do harm. Glasses keep up the strain."

WILLIAM H. BATES, MD

When you first remove your glasses, the world will appear blurred. You may be tempted to put them on again, to see clearly. Every time you do, you delay your progress.

Even just a few minutes of using full-strength glasses can cause you to lose all the improvement you have gained. This lengthens the time it takes you to regain perfect sight. Continued use of full-strength glasses prevents permanent improvement.

When you use glasses, you trade the "cheap thrill" of a sharper image for long-term debility in your vision. Photo by Vicky Hladynets on Unsplash.

When you use glasses, you trade the "cheap thrill" of a sharper image for long-term debility in your vision. Instead of reaching for glasses, reach for one of the vision techniques. These will keep your vision on an upward path.

Lowering Your Glasses Prescription if You Are Near-sighted

If you do NOT have a drivers license restriction for glasses, you can simply discard them.

If you need glasses to drive, you can reduce the prescription so that you are seeing 20/40 instead of 20/20 with the glasses on — or whatever the legal limit for driving is where you live. This fulfills the DMV requirement while at the same time giving you the opportunity to improve your sight.

NOTE: While most areas require 20/40 vision for driving, some locations have different legal requirements. Be sure your glasses give you good enough vision to pass the drivers test where you live. For the United States, you can check the driving requirements here: Legal Limits for Driving

If you are nearsighted, get glasses that allow you to pass the drivers license test. In most places, you can do that with 20/40 vision. Use these glasses for driving, and take then off for everything else. Photo by Md Mahdi on Unsplash.

While 20/40 might not seem like much of a drop in prescription, most nearsighted people find that a 20/40 correction is about 1.00 lower than full strength glasses (so -3.00 instead of -4.00). This varies with people. Your optometrist can measure your vision to determine exactly what prescription gives you driveable vision.

Most people who start with a prescription of -3.00 or less find they need only one weaker pair of glasses in the process of restoring the sight.

This may be the last pair you will ever buy.

IF YOUR GLASSES ARE -4.50 OR HIGHER

When the nearsighted prescription is higher, it usually works best to get a much lower strength of contact lenses, and put -1.50 glasses on top of the contacts when you drive. The two together should give you 20/40 vision — or whatever the legal limit is for driving where you live.

As your vision improves enough so you can drive with just the contacts alone, reduce the contact lens prescription. Repeat until you are down to no lenses at all.

If you have a higher prescription, get a weak pair of contact lenses, and put -1.50 glasses on top when you drive. The two together should give you driveable vision (20/40 in most locales). Photo by Nonsap Visuals on Unsplash

For example: Sharon began in December with a -7.75 prescription. She initially got -5.50 contacts and -1.50 glasses.

As her vision improved, she got new contacts about every six weeks (disposable ones which cost her only $20). By April, she was using -1.25 contacts. By June, she was out of lenses altogether.

If you cannot wear contact lenses, you can get two pairs of glasses — one for driving and one for everything else.

Where can you get a weaker prescription?

Any optometrist can prescribe them, but some are unwilling to do so. You might have to make a few calls to find someone willing to work with you.

As far as purchasing contact lenses and glasses, of course you can get them from any optometrist. You can also buy them online. I do not recommend any particular sites. My students do have favorites, though, and these are:

- Zennioptical.com (glasses)
- Goggles4U.com (glasses)
- contactlenses.co.uk (contact lenses)
- https://www.lenspure.com/ (contact lenses)
- https://www.saveonlens.com (contact lenses)

DID YOU START OUT NEARSIGHTED AND "PROGRESS" TO BIFOCALS LATER IN LIFE?

People wear bifocals for different reasons. You might have been nearsighted all your life, using glasses for seeing in the distance, but later in life you found you could not read with your glasses on — but you can with them off. If this describes you, there are two options:

- Take glasses off to read. This is best if you can do it.
- Lower your nearsighted glasses and contact lens prescription as described previously in this chapter. With reduced strength glasses, most people find they can read perfectly well while wearing the glasses or contacts.

IF YOU USE READING GLASSES

The easiest way to get out of reading glasses is to take the course Improving Close Vision — Read Without Glasses at Any Age and apply the techniques you learn there whenever you read. Most people find they can discard reading glasses after this course.

Improving close vision is relatively easy: Learn how to read without strain, and wean yourself through progressively weaker glasses. Photo by bruce mars on Unsplash.

DID YOU START WITH READING GLASSES AND MOVE INTO BIFOCALS LATER ON?

If this is you, your glasses prescription would have a plus sign in front of the numbers (+1.75, +2.50, for example), and your vision would be better for distance than it is for reading.

If you can drive safely and legally without glasses, you can simply get a weaker pair of glasses for reading, and as your vision improves keep lowering the strength — for example, reducing the strength of the glasses from +2.75 to +2.00, +1.50, +1.00 and then to no glasses.

If you need glasses to drive, get glasses for distance that give you 20/40 vision, or whatever the legal requirement is where you live. Get a stronger pair of glasses for reading — strong enough for you to actually work with them on, but not strong enough for fine print to be clear.

As the vision improves, your driving glasses will become your reading glasses, as you gradually wean yourself from them altogether.

If you use transition glasses as described here, use them only for essential reading (or driving, if you require them for that). Take them off immediately when you look across the room.

PART THREE
DAILY PRACTICE
WHAT TO PRACTICE DAILY AND HOW MUCH TIME TO PRACTICE

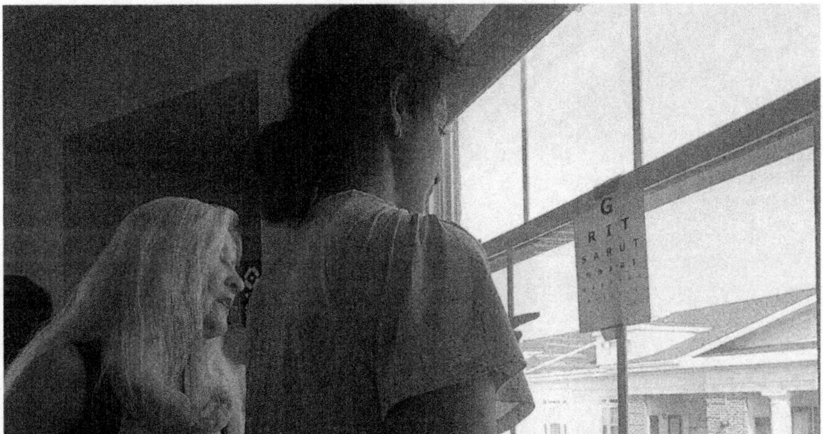

Practice with letters every day to sharpen up your vision. Then apply the same technique(s) throughout the day.

CHAPTER 8
DO THREE THINGS DAILY
TO IMPROVE YOUR EYESIGHT

Shift every day — with the sun when possible, or with a light. Shifting breaks the stare, and turns on your sense of stationary objects moving. Photo by Steven Sprung at stevensprung.com.

You've learned how to replace staring with shifting, see stationary objects moving, letter techniques to improve your vision, and to see without effort from the back of the head with the peripheral vision open.

How do you put it together? What do you practice daily

to turn those quick flashes of clarity into permanently clear vision?

ESSENTIALS: DO THREE THINGS DAILY

1. ***Use a shifter*** or do long swings, 5 - 30 minutes per day.
2. ***See stationary objects moving,*** and / or see from the back of the head and / or open up your peripheral vision. Do this throughout the day while you walk, drive, read, or look at your phone.
3. ***Practice with letters*** to clear up your vision, 5-20 minutes per day. As you get more experience and better results with the letters, take your best technique and apply it throughout the day, instead of (or in addition to) seeing stationary objects moving, opening up the periphery or seeing from the back of the head.

IMPROVING YOUR VISION TAKES EITHER TIME OR ATTENTION

You can improve your eyesight in two different ways: By taking **TIME** out of your day to practice techniques, or by giving your vision **ATTENTION** throughout the day — to see things moving, for example.

Most people combine the two approaches, and do some time-out practice mixed with a lot of moment-to-moment application.

TIME-OUT PRACTICES — ONES THAT REQUIRE TIME OUT OF YOUR DAY TO DO THEM

Time-out practice improves the vision in the sessions, and the improvement carries over to the rest of the day. Time-out exercises are:

- Shifting : 5-10 minutes
- Long swings: 3 minutes (100 swings)
- Letter practice: 5-10 minutes
- Other "time-out" practices are Jin Shin Jyutsu, acupressure, palming, sunning — these are beyond the scope of this book

When you want rapid improvement, you can spend several hours per day practicing these techniques.

At Gloria's 4-Day Super Sight Retreats, participants palm five minutes every hour, use a shifter for 30 minutes twice a day, and spend hours each day in sessions with letters and other objects. This immersion allows students to make as much improvement in four days as it would ordinarily take months to achieve.

MOMENT-TO-MOMENT PRACTICE

Moment-to-moment practice improves the vision throughout the day; the more often you remember to practice, the faster the improvement.

You can apply these type of exercises anywhere, anytime. It doesn't take time, but it does take attention. This approach takes ***attention***. Here are examples of moment-to-moment practices:

- Seeing stationary objects moving
- Opening up the periphery
- Seeing from the back of the head
- See things worse in the periphery

- Also blinking, remembering a swinging point, or imagining a Foundation Object (these techniques are beyond the scope of this book)

GLASSES, PRACTICE AND INTEGRATION

If you stop using glasses, practice hours every day, and spend the rest of the time integrating the techniques, you will get rapid improvement.

On the other hand, if you use the same glasses you have been using, never practice seeing differently, and/or never apply this new way of seeing, your vision will stay the same.

Most people find a happy balance between these two extremes. They lower their prescription, spend 10-20 minutes per day with techniques, and integrate the new way of seeing throughout the day.

CHAPTER 9
A SIMPLE DAILY ROUTINE
THIS CAN ALWAYS BE MODIFIED TO FIT YOUR INDIVIDUAL NEEDS

It's always tricky giving a daily routine, because we live such different lives. A good routine for one person would not work for another. And some people don't do well with routines at all — they respond better by spontaneous, spur-of-the-moment practice throughout the day.

But so many people request a daily practice schedule, I am including one you can use as a framework for your own vision improvement project.

Start your day with shifting.

MORNING — WHEN YOU WAKE UP, DO TWO THINGS

1. Shifting — five minutes in the sun if you can get it, or without, if you can't. This gets your eyes moving for the day.

Option: Do 100 long swings instead.

Option: Sit up in bed and do a slow head swing, eyes open, with and/or without a shifter.

2. Letter-Practice — five to ten minutes with good light, at your favorable distance, using your best technique(s). This not only sharpens your vision, it also makes it easier to keep improving the eyesight throughout the day.

THROUGHOUT THE DAY — DO ONE OF THESE

- See stationary objects moving, or
- See from the back of the head, or
- Keep your peripheral vision open

See stationary objects moving, or be aware of the periphery, or see from the back of the head while you do other activities. Photo by Eugene Chystiakov on Unsplash

See stationary objects moving, or apply one of the other moment-to-moment techniques as you go about your day. These do not take any time out of your day, but you do have to remember to do them.

See if you can remember to see motion (or the periphery, or seeing from the back of the head) at least 30-40 times each day.

Do it while you're on a computer, driving, walking, reading, texting, or doing any other activity.

NIGHT — BEFORE YOU GO TO SLEEP, DO THIS

100 Long Swings — just before you go to sleep. This sends you to bed with your eyes shifting, so you get six to eight hours of free practice while you sleep.

End your day with the long swing, just before you go to sleep. It sends you to sleep with your eyes shifting, and gives you six to eight hours of free practice.

PART FOUR
BONUS MATERIALS - LETTER-CARDS AND MORE

CHAPTER 10

HOW THE EYES FOCUS

WHAT HAPPENS PHYSICALLY WHEN THE EYES FOCUS — AND WHEN THEY DON'T

The eyes focus automatically where the mind is focused. Every single time. Photo by Marina Vitale on Unsplash

What causes the eye to focus at one distance or another? Can the eye decide where to look? No. The eyes focus where the mind is focused.

The instant you shift your attention, the eyes will change shape to adjust their focus. The muscles that change the focus of the eye are involuntary: You don't have to tell your heart to beat — the heart muscle is controlled involuntarily.

This also true for the eye: Imagine if you had to consciously focus your eyes all day long: "OK, focus here. Now focus over there." What a mess that would be! The focusing of the eye is automatic, involuntary. The eyes focus where the mind is focused at any given moment.

Physically, the eyes adjust their focus by adjusting the tension on six muscles on the outside of the eye. As soon as your attention shifts from one detail to another, the brain sends a command through the nerves to the muscles, telling them to adjust their tension.

The eyes don't have a choice; they focus automatically, exactly where the attention is.

That's why glasses, contact lenses and surgery are so unsatisfactory: They only treat the symptom — the eye being in the wrong shape. Because the strain continues, the vision keeps getting worse.

To make permanent improvement, the underlying cause of imperfect sight must be eliminated: *the unconscious mental strain to see,* which pulls the eye out of focus.

NEARSIGHTEDNESS (SHORT-SIGHTEDNESS, MYOPIA)

Nearsightedness is caused by keeping your eyes in a close focus when looking into the distance. Children often do this in a classroom: They make an effort, mentally, to bring the information in close to see it. This causes two things to happen

1. The eye stays in a close focus, where the mind is, even when looking in the distance.
2. The image appears larger than it really is. Why? Because when you focus close, objects appear larger than they do in the distance. Nearsighted lenses compensate by shrinking the image, making it smaller. With nearsighted lenses, you can see far away while your eyes remain focused close up.

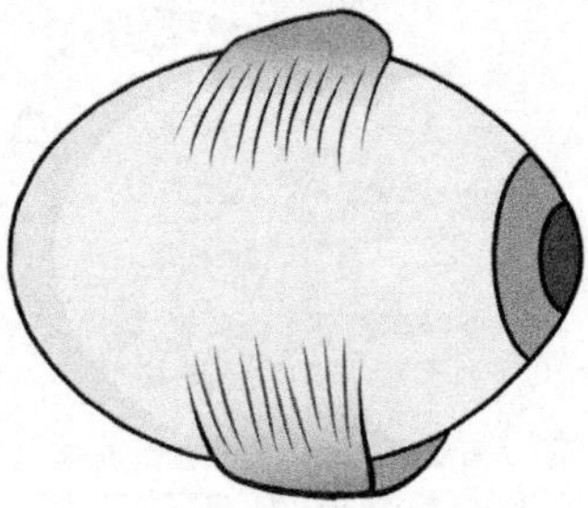

***Close Focus**: These two muscles contract to focus the eye close up. They stay tense when the eye is nearsighted.*

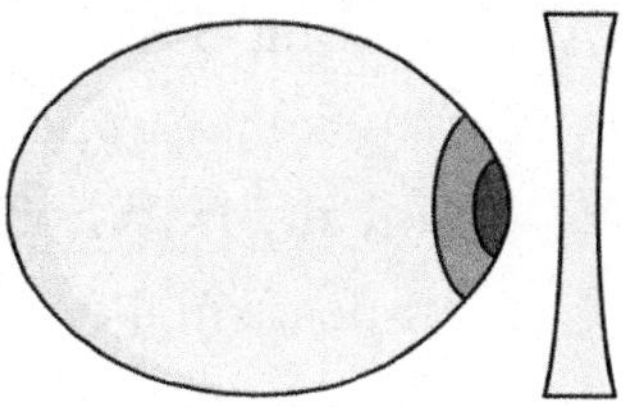

***Nearsighted glasses** allow you to see in the distance with your eye focused close up. Unfortunately, you have to keep you eyes in a close focus to see far away through the glasses.*

To see through nearsighted glasses, you have to keep your eyes focused close up. The glasses lock in the strain and make it habitual.

FARSIGHTEDNESS (LONG-SIGHTEDNESS, HYPERMETROPIA, PRESBYOPIA)

Farsightedness is caused by keeping your eyes in a far focus when looking close up. You often see farsighted people pushing things away to see them. Instead of the attention coming in close, there is an effort to push the object away.

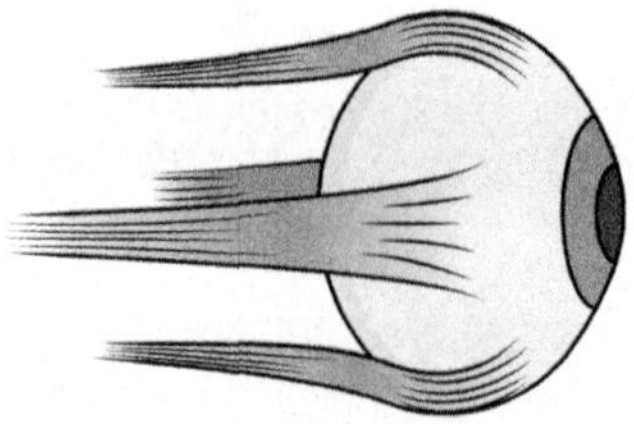

Far Focus: These four muscles contract to focus the eye far away. They stay tense when the eye is farsighted.

This causes two things to happen:

1. The eye stays in a far focus, where the mind is, even when looking close.
2. The image appears smaller than it really is. Why? Because objects appear smaller far away than they do close up. Farsighted glasses compensate by magnifying the image, making it appear larger. The glasses enable you to see close up with the eye focused in the distance.

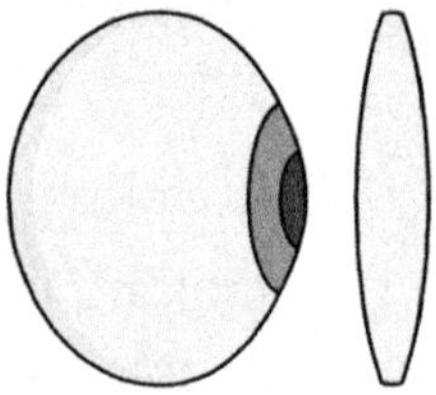

***Farsighted glasses** allow you to see close with your eye focused in the distance. Unfortunately, you have to keep you eyes in a far focus to see close through the glasses.*

To see through farsighted glasses, you must keep your eyes in a far focus — even when looking close. This locks in the strain and makes it habitual.

Astigmatism: *There is an unequal tension on the six muscles that focus the eye. This is caused by a confusion as to where you are focused.*

ASTIGMATISM

Astigmatism is caused by a confusion where the focus is. This sends mixed signals to the eye, which attempts to focus at more than one distance at the same time.

The unequal tension on the muscles pulls the eye into a lopsided shape.

Glasses compensate by bending the light rays so they focus through the distortion. To see through astigmatic glasses, you have to maintain the unequal tension continuously.

GLASSES LOCK IN THE STRAIN

To see through glasses, you have to keep your eyes in the same shape they were in when the glasses were prescribed. This makes the vision problem habitual.

CHAPTER 11
A BRIEF HISTORY OF NATURAL VISION IMPROVEMENT

The first case of myopia (nearsightedness) was corrected in 1896. It's been more than 100 years since this method was first introduced to the world. Yet due to suppression, professional jealousy, greed and prejudice, it has largely been kept from the eyes of the general population.

It wasn't always that way. When the method was first developed, it was reviewed in medical journals and discussed in magazines such as *Hearst's International* and *Scientific American*.

> The *Journal of the Allied Medical Association* described Dr. Bates' method as "An equally fascinating and overwhelmingly conclusive record of the accomplishments, in actual cures of defective vision."

Public schools in New York, Connecticut and New Jersey

used this method for over 15 years to prevent myopia from developing, with a 71% success rate.

ITS SUCCESS WAS ITS DOWNFALL

Its success was its downfall. Doctors feared for their position, for the approach flew in the face of all they believed to be true. Opticians feared for their business. And so, the method was carefully ignored, silently passed over, by the professional world at large.

Except for a few, who carried the light of truth to future generations.

WILLIAM H. BATES, M.D.

William Horatio Bates, M.D.

The first man to correct eyesight without glasses was William H. Bates, an ophthalmologist (eye surgeon) who graduated from Cornell University in 1881 and the College of Physicians and Surgeons in 1885.

Dr. Bates was the attending physician at the Manhattan Eye and Ear Hospital, and also practiced at Bellevue Hospital, New York infirmary and Northeastern Dispensary.

He was an ophthalmology instructor at the New York Post-graduate Medical school, 1886 - 91.

In 1894, as a result of his research into the ductless glands, Dr. Bates discovered the substance that today is known as adrenaline. He developed the surgical technique for Radial Keratotomy (RK), the pre-cursor to Lasik. Doctors today embrace the concept which Dr. Bates developed and then rejected over 100 years ago.

Dr. Bates went on to develop a system of restoring eyesight that is nonsurgical, noninvasive, and effects a permanent cure, according to the actual records on file of thousands of his patients.

When he discovered that the cause of refractive errors is functional instead of medical, he trained both doctors and lay people in his method.

MARGARET D. CORBETT

Margaret D. Corbett

Dr. Bates cured Margaret Corbett's husband of blindness. In gratitude, she devoted the rest of her life to helping others improve their vision.

She studied with Dr. Bates, became a teacher of his method, and opened a school in Los Angeles where, at one time, she had over 40 teachers actively teaching vision improvement. One of her most famous students was Aldous Huxley.

As her reputation for improving eyesight grew, she incurred the jealous wrath of local eye doctors.

> "In 1930, she was brought into court by the organized optometrists and ophthalmologists of Southern California on the charge of 'practicing medicine and optometry without a license.'
>
> "More than 500 of her grateful clients in Los Angeles alone volunteered to testify for her. Her witnesses included notable writers, screen stars and social leaders." [*The case was dismissed.*]
>
> NATIONAL CYCLOPEDIA OF AMERICAN BIOGRAPHY

In 1940, a bill was introduced in the California state legislature to ban the Bates method. Margaret Corbett took witnesses to the senate committee hearings, and gave lessons to senators and their wives. Due to her efforts, the measure was defeated in the Senate after it had passed in the Assembly.

VISION IMPROVEMENT TODAY

In 1978, Gloria Ginn was certified as an instructor in the Bates method. She then sought out the "old-timers" such as Elin Gilbert in Seattle and Miss Sage in London, England, who at ages 76 and 78, respectively, could see 20/20 and read microprint without glasses.

Her teachers gave her documents by Dr. Bates which opened the door to a whole new understanding as to how Dr. Bates restored eyesight so consistently and quickly.

While studying in England with Miss Sage, Gloria spent

over six hours per day at the British Museum Library, and then later at the Library of Congress in Washington D.C., researching and documenting vision improvement methods of Dr. Bates and his successors.

During 42 years of full-time teaching and over 55,000 hours of study and research, Gloria has discovered certain keys which literally turn on vision.

She founded the School of Better Eyesight in 1978, and brought it online in 2019.

CHAPTER 12

CHARTS AND PRACTICE MATERIALS

FEEL FREE TO MAKE COPIES OF THE CHARTS AND PRACTICE MATERIALS IN THIS CHAPTER — FOR YOUR PERSONAL USE ONLY. NO COMMERCIAL USE, PLEASE.

Y O U

S E E

B E S T B Y

M A K I N G

N O E F F O R T

I M A G I N E M O R E

D E T A I L I N

A L L Y O U S E E

G

R I T

S A R U T

N B A R I

D A B F T G C

O K I F L E A

G E T E E R T

CAN YOU FIND THE SEVEN ANIMALS ?

L B O

O A R

A Q N A P

P U A N E

P A N G A

L T A E C

E □ △ X H

CAN YOU FIND THE FIVE FRUITS ?

Fundamentals

by

William H. Bates, M.D.

1. Glasses discarded permanently.

2. **Central Fixation is seeing best where you are looking.**

3. Favorable conditions: Light may be bright or dim. The distance of the print from the eyes, where seen best, also varies with people.

4. Shifting: With normal sight the eyes are moving all the time.

5. Swinging: When the eyes move slowly or rapidly from side to side, stationary objects appear to move in the opposite direction.

6. Long Swing: Stand with the feet about one foot apart. Turn the body to the right, at the same time lifting the heel of the left foot. Do not move the head or eyes or pay any attention to the apparent movement of stationary objects. Now place the left heel on the floor, turn the body to the left, raising the heel of the right foot. Alternate.

7. Drifting Swing: When practicing this swing, one pays no attention to the clearness of stationary objects, which appear to be moving. The eyes wander from point to point slowly, easily, or lazily, so that the stare or strain may be avoided.

8. Variable Swing: Hold the forefinger of one hand six inches from the right eye and about the same distance to the right. Look straight ahead and move the head a short distance from side to side. The finger appears to move.

9. Stationary Objects Moving: By moving the head and eyes a short distance from side to side, being sure to blink, one can imagine stationary objects to be moving.

10. Memory: Improving the memory of letters or other objects improves the vision for everything.

11. Imagination: We see only what we think we see, or what we imagine. We can only imagine what we remember.

12. Rest: All cases of imperfect sight are improved by closing the eyes and resting them.

13. Palming: The closed eyes may be covered with the palm of one or both hands.

14. Blinking: The normal eye blinks, or closes and opens very frequently.

15. Mental Pictures: As long as one is awake, one has all kinds of mental pictures. If these pictures are remembered easily, perfectly, the vision is benefited.

CHAPTER 13

DID YOU LIKE THIS BOOK?

Your review — even just one or two lines — is critical for helping new readers discover me. I read all my reviews and would love to hear from you!

Here's a link to go directly to the review box on amazon: http://www.amazon.com/review/create-review?&asin=B09LKH7794

But if you'd rather, reviews are welcome on any site where you purchase books!

Thank you!

Gloria

NOTES

FOREWORD

1. Nearly all vision improvement systems today had their beginnings with the work of **William H. Bates, M.D.**, an ophthalmologist who lived from 1860 to 1931. He published a book, *The Cure of Imperfect Sight by Treatment Without Glasses*, in 1919. **Margaret D. Corbett** was trained by Dr. Bates and further developed and taught his method. She published three books: One of the most known is *Help Yourself to Better Sight*.

ABOUT THE AUTHOR

As the foremost authority in natural vision improvement, Gloria Ginn is sought internationally as a speaker and advisor. She is the founder of the School of Better Eyesight, where — since 1978 — she has helped thousands of people improve their eyesight and regain 20/20 vision.

ALSO BY GLORIA GINN

Free Your Mind to Improve Your Eyesight

The Super Sight Papers

How To Read Small Print Without Glasses at Any Age

School of Better Eyesight Comprehensive Guide — a nine part series available exclusively with membership in the Super Sight Squad™

ACKNOWLEDGMENTS

This book could not have happened without the many mentors and students in my life. There isn't space to acknowledge all of you by name, which I would love to do.

Here are a few of those who have been exceptionally helpful in my understanding and development of this method:

MY MENTORS:

- Dr. Jerianne Tabor, my first vision teacher, who also trained me as an instructor in vision improvement.
- Elin Gilbert, who taught me the meaning of "wonderment" and gave me my first copies of Dr. Bates' Better Eyesight Magazine — which I had not known existed.
- Miss Sage, my dear British teacher who was so generous with her time — and even opened her attic to me so I could read letters and writings she had collected about Dr. Bates and his method.
- Eldene Dutton, Jerianne's teacher, who invited me into her home and opened my eyes to a whole new

body of knowledge.

- Mary Burmeister, my beloved Jin Shin Jyutsu teacher who "walked her talk" when she said, "Only those who see the invisible can do the impossible." Her life's work continues to touch thousands of people today. My life is enriched, and my students today benefit tremendously from her mentorship.
- Don Ginn, my former husband, who introduced me to Jerianne and pushed me to become both a vision teacher and a Jin Shin Jyutsu practitioner. He accompanied me to meet Elin Gilbert, and called me from England after meeting Miss Sage, to say: "You need to put everything on hold and come here for the summer to study with her." He was by my side when I taught my first two groups of vision teachers, in 1985 and 1986, and I probably would not have become a teacher without his influence.
- Georgi Lozanov, one of the most amazing teachers and innovators I have even known. I am grateful to have jumped on the opportunity to study with him, if just for a long weekend in Seattle with other educators.

MY STUDENTS AND FRIENDS, TO WHOM I OWE SO MUCH

I have often said, "My students have been my greatest teachers." And it's true.

From the early days in Redwood Shores with Colleen, David, John, Marilyn — and so many more, to today with Chaniece, Holly, Patricia, Sapna, Rita, Steven, Ira, Marlon, Sarah, Juliana, Mary, Debra, Alka, Jessica, Vandana, Vimala, Sathish, Sally — and thousands more — you have been my inspiration, my driving force, and my greatest joy.

- A special thanks to Rita, who won't stop booking seminars for me. She and her husband Steve have become the best of friends.
- Also to Steven who so graciously filmed an entire four day retreat in 2019 — the first (but not the last) time I had ever allowed myself to be filmed in action. Until then, my words lived only in my writings, and in the lives of all those who had been my students. Steven encouraged my initial attempts to learn the internet — even giving me an old ipad — my first. He and his partner Victor will always be dear to my heart.
- I want to acknowledge my sister, Marlene, for being my original role model and best friend. (She still is.) Her accomplishments are too numerous to recount here, but on a personal level her creativity, love, determination and friendship inspire me every day.
- Thanks to Ira for being so generous with his amazing knowledge of computers, and his patience as I came into the 21st Century. He taught me how to make a link out of a website address, how to get the "mail" function working on my desktop — and

how to use a cell phone. He painstakingly scanned files of written testimonials I had gathered from students, over the years. And he always asks the best questions.

- Mary: Her positive outlook and penetrating questions forced me to conceptualize what I actually do with my students that causes them to get results.
- Then there's Beverly — who started as a student, became the best of friends, and is now an invaluable associate. Her quiet, calm, graceful presence soothes my soul.
- Juliana from CalTech, with her brilliant mind, took what I taught her and put it into action — wearing out my little booklets by using them so much. She cured her cataract, brought up the vision in an eye that had endured a detached retina, and stimulated me to create variations on my fusion techniques that have been breakthroughs. Juliana also generously opened her stunning mountain ranch to host two vision retreats.

I could write a book about each and every one of my students: each of you who have been my private students, or attended a Super Sight Seminar, a Super Sight retreat, or an EyeExcel clinic — and each of you who participated in a 21 day challenge, an online course, or the Inner Circle.

You are my inspiration and my driving force. You are why I keep growing, keep developing, keep learning better ways to improve eyesight. Thank you.

Printed in Great Britain
by Amazon

58307522R00089